Cricket XXXX Cricket

Frances Edmonds was educated at the Ursuline Convent, Chester, and New Hall, Cambridge, graduating in 1973 with an M.A. (Hons) in Modern Languages, and humorous tendencies in French, Italian and Spanish as well as English.

She then trained as a conference interpreter, and worked on the Commission of European Communities in Brussels for four years before returning to England to marry cricketer Phil Edmonds. She has been profoundly uninterested in cricket ever since.

Frances now travels worldwide as a freelance conference interpreter, writes for *The Times*, and is a regular contributor to Radio 4's *Loose Ends*. In her spare time she likes drinking vintage champagne and inventing new words for the English language.

Frances Edmonds

CRICKET XXXX CRICKET

Pan Books
in association with Heinemann

First published 1987 by The Kingswood Press
This edition published 1988 by Pan Books Ltd,
Cavaye Place, London SW10 9PG
in association with Heinemann
9 8 7 6 5 4 3 2 1
© Frances Edmonds 1987
ISBN 0 330 30351 1
Printed in Great Britain by Richard Clay Ltd.

For my mother, Patricia

Contents

Acknowledgements

AUSTRALIA

Carol Bennetto – William Heinemann
Sandy Grant – MD, William Heinemann
Eileen 'Red' Bond
David Michael – Bond Corporation, Australia
Jane Adams – News Corporation Ltd
Mark Hopkinson – Schroder's Australia Ltd
Carol Aamodt – News Hyatt Hotel, Sydney
Rod and Fran Lugton – William Heinemann
Queensland and Torres Strait Islander Consultative Committee (QUATSICC)
Robert Mayne *et al* – Thomas Hardy & Sons Pty. Ltd
Andrew 'Spud' Spedding (and *White Crusader*) – Shore Manager of the British challenge for the America's Cup, Fremantle
Channel 10's *Good Morning, Australia* team, Sydney
Brendan and Pat Redden, Melbourne
Bollinger champagne
Ansett Airlines

IN ENGLAND

Mark Lucas and Virginia Allan – Fraser & Dunlop Scripts
Tom Clarke – Sports Editor, *The Times*
Castlemaine XXXX – Allied Lyons
Johnnie Walker whisky and Hine cognac
Margot Richardson – Kingswood Press
Rachel Ward Lilley – Kingswood Press
Derek Wyatt – Kingswood Press
Bill Bell – copy-editor
Kate Gay – British Airways
Francis de Souza – British Airways
David Hooper – Biddle & Co
Adrian Murrell – All-Sport

AND ESPECIALLY

PHILIPPE-HENRI EDMONDS – whose sleeping patterns ensure that
there are enough hours in the day.

Glossary

Although I have made every effort to write this diary in English, my trusty copy-editor has pointed out various instances of linguistic interference. This is no doubt due to a protracted period of exposure to the local Australian patois, 'Strine'.

Here, in non-alphabetical order, are a few of the most common colloquial expressions assimilated:

Stubbies	Small receptacles for beer or lager
Tinnies	Large receptacles for beer or lager
Eskies	Large receptacles for stubbies or tinnies
Akubra	Type of hat worn by a Crocodile Dundee
Crocodile Dundee	Type of man who wears an Akubra hat
Scam	Fraud
Banana benders	Queenslanders
Larrikin	Yobbo
Ratted	Inebriated
To chunder	To perform a 'pavement pizza', a 'technicolour yawn': to be sick

| Vegemite | Essential element of Australian staple diet: a vegetable extract-based version of Marmite |
| Funnelweb spider | One of Australia's most dangerous arachnida |

Preface

Never ever believe anything you read in the newspapers. Believe me, I know what I'm talking about. On occasion I write for them.

Take conference interpreting, for example. That certainly is not all it is cracked up to be. It is not all duty-free Hermes scarves and Chanel No.5; jet-setting around the world making boring, banal, superficial and ill-formed politicians sound riveting, innovative, outstanding and brill . . . or, indeed, from time to time, vice versa.

No. Sometimes you come across the real thing, the people who *really* know what they are talking about, the experts. And inevitably, when you do, they are talking about something incomprehensibly esoteric, such as plasma physics, and when they are it is in exotic locations such as a laboratory in Culham, not a million miles away from such exciting railway stations as Didcot.

Not that nuclear fusion is not a fascinating topic, on the contrary. And not that the relative merits of Ion Cyclotron Resonance heating, Lower Hybrid Resonance heating, Electron Cyclotron Resonance Heating, Alfren Wave Heating, Turbulent Heating and Adiabatic heating are not subjects worthy of protracted ponder on a cold, misty October afternoon. Dear me, no.

It may, perhaps, have had more to do with the cumulative

effects of a pharmaceutical conference in Portsmouth the week prior, epitomized in awfulness by a Spaniard with a cleft palate, semi-intelligible in five Community languages, telling us all about benzodiazepene in his own highly individualistic brand of French. That, and the conference a fortnight before in Milan, an unspeakable meeting on pre-impregnated gas-pressure assisted cables, dominated by an unstoppable flow of manic Italians – that was probably what did it.

My thoughts turned to the workers on the other side of the world: to the old man, stretched out on a beach on the Gold Coast, exhausted after a heavy thirty minutes turning his arm over in the nets.

I rang my travel agent in London, and booked myself a seat on the next flight to Australia.

1

The ex-Prime Minister's trousers

I must admit to being somewhat miffed. No, not somewhat. That is far too pusillanimous an adverb to convey my current state of displeasure. Extremely.

You have all, no doubt, heard the story of 'The Emperor's New Clothes'. Of course you have. Even people educated in Queensland have heard the story of the Emperor's new clothes. Well, my arrival in Australia has been totally upstaged by a better one than that: two television and three radio interviews cancelled – and all because of the saga of 'The Ex-Prime Minister's Old Trousers'.

Former Australian Prime Minister, Malcolm ('Rectitude' *used* to be my middle name) Fraser, has been very busy on the after-dinner speaking circuit since his elevation to Chairman of the Eminent Persons Group. The EPG is an eclectic selection of sometime somebodies and current busybodies, mandated by Commonwealth leaders to report on the South African problem in general and apartheid in particular. Australia, with its erstwhile 'Whites Only' immigration policy, and a healthy track record in wiping out its own indigenous Aboriginal population, was the obvious country to field a Chairperson for such an egregious body.

Malcolm was back, if not centre stage, then at least in the wings of international diplomacy.

It was therefore a trifle unfortunate, after one such speaking assignment in Memphis, Tennessee, that Mr Fraser should somehow lose his trousers, his wallet, and his diplomatic passport during a nocturnal sojourn at the Admiral Benbow Motel. The Admiral Benbow Motel, according to Memphis Tennessee Tourist Board officials more inured to dealing with Elvis Presley groupies wetting their pants rather than ex-Prime Ministers losing them, is a perfectly – almost totally – respectable hotel. Not quite the sort of establishment in which you would expect an eminent person to lay his weary wallet and diplomatic passport, but the right side of kosher at least. What does seem extremely odd about the place is that it would not appear to provide telephones in the bedrooms. Why on earth, otherwise, would the debagged ex-premier arrive *in eminenta persona* at the reception desk to report the loss, with only a towel to swathe his lower regions – hardly a step designed to ward off unwelcome publicity from the probing eye of the world's media? Another mystery is why Mr Fraser would sign himself into the good Admiral's residence as one 'Joan Jones'. 'We thought Joan was the Australian way of spelling John,' obfuscated the motel's receptionist nicely. With such a thorough grasp of international diplomacy, maybe *she* should be chairing the Eminent Persons Group.

Australian marketing men recognize a good wheeze when they see one, and a Melbourne men's underwear company is already advertising extra-durable, guaranteed against holes, executive underpants, just in case *you* ever get caught with *your* pants down. Whatever happened to good taste? At all events, the episode does not appear to have ruined the elder statesman's hitherto unsullied reputation. On the contrary, informed pundits who believe that Malcolm's stiff-and-starchy never-put-a-foot-wrong image won him little sympathy Down Under are now convinced that this rather louche little episode could herald a complete renaissance of his political career. Yes, folks, Cecil Parkinson would assuredly have been better off in Australia, and so, for that matter, am I. The end of October in England, when the clocks go back, and the nights close in at 5 o'clock, is the most depressing time of the year, and five months in the Antipodean sunshine seems no bad way to spend an English winter. I arrived in Adelaide on 31 October, three weeks after the England cricket team had left our green and pleasant land in an all-out effort to continue the glorious summer game in warmer climes, to retain the Ashes, and to break the spell of disasters which has dogged them since their disastrous tour of the West Indies in early 1986. A home season spent losing to the Indians and New Zealanders has done little to revive confidence, or restore morale, and all-rounder Ian Botham's subsequent exclusion from the team on drugs offences was, perhaps excessively, sorely felt.

The British Airways inaugural flight from London to Adelaide was twenty-seven hours of complete relaxation. Unlike most people, I thoroughly enjoy long-haul flights. Responsibility for your own life is wrested from you for the duration, and all you can do is sit back, and relax. One of the stewardesses on the London/Bangkok sector was the ex-wife of Geoff Howarth, former captain of New Zealand, but as a tribute to her sheer professionalism on a chock-a-block flight, she only managed to come and chat to me when the plane had actually landed. It was another of those sad tales of cricketing marriages, where long and enforced absences create a gradual and irretrievable breakdown. It is nevertheless the number of such marriages that survive that continues to surprise me, not the number that fail.

As the plane circled to land in Adelaide, rows upon rows of Formula One racing cars hove into view, like so many multi-coloured Dinky toys, waiting to be freighted back to their respective workshops. The entire city, hitherto better known for its multiplicity of churches, was still in the throes of post-Grand Prix euphoria. With the few exceptions of people who objected to the inevitable traffic jams, the noise, and the influx of the racing world's ritzy razzamatazz, the majority of the good burghers of Adelaide had been immersed in the hopes of Britain's Nigel Mansell, and his bid for the World Championship. Mansell had only to secure third place in the race, and the title would have been his. Tragically, his aspirations burst along with his left rear tyre, and he narrowly escaped with his life. Alain Prost carried off the Championship. But, in all honesty, who cares? Alain Prost is not an Englishman.

The flight had been full as far as Sydney, but we who emerged at the final destination, 'The City of Churches and Light', were few. My copious amounts of baggage arrived almost immediately, thanks to the special ministrations of British Airways Special Services Executive, Francis de Souza. The cricket team had flown out heavily subsidized by British Airways, but the national flagcarrier's well-tapped munificence even embraces sports less familiar, and the British challenge in the America's Cup is also being generously sponsored by the self-confessed World's Favourite Airline. Francis's VIP attentions are reserved not merely for the superstars, but even extend to the vicarious extrusions of same, the wives, and I was unreservedly grateful for the 'hand' with my twenty kilos of excess baggage. Most of this comprised gear my husband, spin-bowler Phil, had failed to remember, items any professional cricketer could easily forget: cricket trousers, thigh pads, cricket shirts, England sweaters, spikes, helmet, an extra bat, chest pad, you know, all those relatively redundant peripherals to a four-month tour of Australia.

Hypnotizing myself into a Bob Willis-genre catatonic trance, watching other people's luggage swirl around on the black, rubber carousel, I noticed gossip columnist Auberon Waugh. His avuncular physiognomy belies his often gloriously malicious mind. He is the sort of elegantly satirical, brilliantly vituperative, unashamed misogynist, whose tripe-writer ribbons mere part-time mickey-takers, such as myself, are unworthy to change.

Had he been sent here to report, in his inimitably excori-

ating fashion, on the 'Clashes for the Ashes'? I savoured
the thought. Sadly not. The distinguished progeny of the
author of *Brideshead Revisited, Scoop* and *Black Mischief*
had been invited to Adelaide in his capacity as wine
connoisseur extraordinaire. An indignant Australian senator
was so incensed when Waugh failed sufficiently to differen-
tiate between South Australian and Hunter Valley wines in
his essays on the Australian grape, she invited him over to
rectify any confusion. I should like to put it on record here
and now (just in case the good senator is reading) that I too
am rather hazy on the organoleptic nuances of said varieties,
and would be perfectly delighted to have my confusion
dispelled as well.

I was met at the airport by a correspondent from the
local press, who inquired whether I would be joining the
team on its forthcoming up-country match in Kalgoorlie.
Kalgoorlie is celebrated throughout Australia for its gold
mines, and for that apparently indispensable adjunct to
towns where lonesome men get too rich, too quick: its
brothels. Unfortunately, the logistics of taking in the forthcoming Melbourne Cup *and* making it up to this indubit-
ably colourful fixture were too awkward to contemplate,
and I had elected to go for the former.

'I'd rather go to the Melbourne Cup,' I explained to the
baby hackette in a jet-lagged attempt at flippancy, 'you get
a better class of horse.'

This did not net me too many friends amongst the
doyennes of Melbourne society, where it was widely and
faithfully misreported as 'a better class of whore'. If the
press *want* you to be outspoken, you can bet your bottom,
devalued Australian dollar, you are *going* to be outspoken.

I arrived at the new and commensurately sumptuous
Adelaide Hilton. It was midday, and Phil was playing at
the Oval in the State match against South Australia.

He had remembered. There, in the bedroom, on top of
the television, lovingly juxtaposed between a pile of *laun-
dered* (at least we're making progress) jockstraps and cricket
socks, was a floral display. Nothing too ostentatious, mind

you. No, indeed on reflection about exactly the same size as the floral displays ubiquitously dotted throughout the entire hotel. And the same selection. 'Happy 10th Anniversary, darling', it proclaimed, in suitably non-person specific terms of endearment. It was signed 'P. H. EDMONDS'.

I was appropriately overwhelmed, and reflected that even if Philippe-Henri had forgotten how to sign his name in anything other than autograph, room-service or credit-card fashion, at least he had remembered that it was ten years since the outbreak of inter-Edmonds hostilities. Ten years and one day, to be exact. I had left England on the 29th of October, and arrived in Australia on the 31st of October. Somewhere in between a twenty-seven-hour international flight and an eight-hour time difference, the 30th of October, the actual day of the original mental aberration, had been lost, snaffled up by the lines of longitude.

Well, the darling boy, whose memory is about as good as Kurt Waldheim's when it comes to remembering emotional occasions which involve expenditure on small tokens of undying love and affection, had at least not forgotten this decadal notch on the yardstick of conjugal bliss. I have to admit that underneath this taut exterior of armadillo-feminism, I had been missing him.

'And I've been missing you too,' he admitted, in one of those intimate moments when, according to women's magazines, men are supposed to tell you you're wonderful, beautiful, adorable, desirable, etc. 'There's been nobody here to aggravate me.'

The tour so far has been fairly eventless. The management's blanket ban on players writing, broadcasting or giving interviews to the press has resulted in fairly lacklustre, if occasionally critical, media coverage. Every member of the press corps shall henceforth be receiving exactly the same statement from the manager, Peter Lush, the assistant manager, Micky Stewart, or the captain, Mike Gatting. According to many of the hardened journos who have already decided to dispense with the press conferences, the 'Gattysburg Addresses' (as the captain's desperately non-sensational, well-coached, and relentlessly innocuous statements have been christened), are 'basically tremendously wise'. There is a lot of 'cricket-wise', 'batting-wise', 'bowling-wise', 'Ashes-wise', 'fielding-wise', and 'practice-wise', together with a 'tremendous' amount of 'basically'. Gatt, patently, has assimilated the art of saying much which means nothing; with such a thorough grasp of international diplomacy, maybe *he* should be chairing the Eminent Persons Group.

No, there has been little yet of the ex-Miss Barbados variety of copy for the press to get hot in the word processor over. There have been a few up-country matches, one in Bundaberg against a Queensland Country XI where the odd bottle of the notorious local rum was dutifully downed, one in Lawes against S. E. Queensland Country, and another against a South Australia XI at Wudinna which was rather more colourful. The tiny plane chartered for the flight from Adelaide hit a storm, and pavement pizzas of the on-going variety were in fairly generalized production throughout the England camp. The manager, Peter Lush, was even fined by the team's social committee for succumbing like the rest. At the back of the plane, not entirely unamused by their faint-hearted Pommie team-mates' gastro-enterological turmoil, sat the non-pukers, Zambian Edmonds, and South African Allan Lamb – iron constitutions, these colonials.

It would be hard work not to like Allan Lamb, and he certainly rates as one of most people's favourite tourists. I have never met anyone with quite as much energy, merriment and good-humoured mischief in him.

At the very beginning of the tour, five of the team – John Emburey, Ian Botham, David Gower, Phil and Allan Lamb – took a seaplane excursion off the coast of Queensland. Thus confined, there was not a lot anybody could do when 'Beefy' Botham took the controls, other than stare hopefully at the aquatic environment, and say a few earnest prayers. Starboard, they noticed a pelican, following them with interest. Suddenly the bird started to hover, its beady eye focused meaningfully. Finally, with an unerring sense of direction, it swooped on its unsuspecting prey, engulfing the unfortunate creature in its capacious mouth. 'Henri!' shouted Lamby to my husband. 'Looks like Frances has arrived!'

Lamby and David Gower seem closer than ever on this trip. In bygone days, Botham and former England captain, 'una tantum' assistant manager, Bob Willis, made up the Gang of Four. Willis, after England's last disastrous tour to the West Indies, is no longer administratively with us, whilst Botham seems to be keeping very much to himself, and his Australian promotions agent. This leaves the Allan and David duo together, as tour veterans of many years' standing.

David, whom Lamb has nicknamed 'Shaggy', a not entirely inappropriate sobriquet, designed to convey the deep-pile carpet effect of David's unruly, blond curls, seems lost. It is received wisdom that I have all the maternal instincts of a Funnelweb spider, but I do have an extremely soft spot for David.

Last year had been such a traumatic year for him. An only child, whose father died many years ago, it came as a body-blow when his mother died weeks before the England team set off to the West Indies. That uncompromisingly dreadful tour ensued, and David, as captain, was inevitably first in the media firing line when it came to handing out the brickbats: no team discipline; want of application; lack of leadership; failure to implement anything even vaguely analogous to a strategy, and so on. He took it all with that indefatigable good humour and charm which uninformed pundits often perceive as indifference. It must be difficult for captains in adversity to know quite how to react to the cricket world's vultures in the face of unremitting criticism. Some, such as ex-Australian captain, Kim Hughes, break down and cry. Some, such as current Australian captain, Allan Border, become uncommunicative, refuse to field press questions, threaten to resign, and earn the nickname 'Grumpy'. Throughout the press onslaught David remained his own laid-back, superficially insouciant self. However, absence of overt, aggressive histrionics drove the blood-lusters even wilder. Any lay person, picking up a British newspaper during that period, would have been forgiven for believing that David had done something rather ill-defined, but nevertheless deeply reprehensible. What in truth he had done was to lose to the best team on earth in its own Caribbean back yard. No one else, in the circumstances, could have done a better job. The noose, however, was already around his neck, and he was given but a short-term, probationary home captaincy against the Indians the following summer.

The rest is history. Chairman of Selectors, Peter May, who has done for the art of communication what Benson and Hedges have done for world health, summarily dismissed David after the first-Test defeat at Lord's. It is, not, as the old adage runs, what you do, it's the way that you do it, and the many people who have grown to admire and respect David will never forget the ungracious ineptitude with which he was given the push.

Vice-captain Mike Gatting was duly appointed captain in his place. Mike, who had had his nose broken by Malcolm Marshall in the first one-day International in Jamaica, had returned to the West Indies to play in only one Test match, the last. *His* reputation, therefore, if not his good looks, had managed to survive the Caribbean experience intact.

The choice of England vice-captain for the home series proved conclusively, to me at least, that certain cricketers' peccadillos are far more easily forgiven than others. Graham Gooch, who, having led a rebel tour to South Africa, spent much of his time in the West Indies feeling mortally aggrieved that a few black politicians should make a few moral points about 'Judas money', had finally to be persuaded forcibly to stay on the tour at all. Donald Carr, then secretary of the Test and County Cricket Board (TCCB), was obliged to fly out to Trinidad after the fourth Test to convince Graham to continue on to the final Test in Antigua. Who will ever know what was said or promised?

Suffice it to say that the man who led a breakaway rebel tour to South Africa, the man who was not entirely sure whether or not he ever wanted to be on tour in the West Indies, the man who subsequently decided that he was not available to tour Australia, was nevertheless granted the honour of the vice-captaincy of England. David Gower, meanwhile, was left completely out in the cold.

And that is how things stand at the moment. David, who has three full tours of Australia to his name, who has more Test experience than the entire touring selection committee put together, has not even been made a selector. There is fairly generalized outrage in the roving press corps at this glaring, almost insulting omission. It is interesting, is it not, how a certain ineffable sense of fair play tends to triumph in the British media? Once a chap has been trampled on sufficiently, suddenly everybody decides it is high time to rehabilitate him. Erstwhile hatchet-job men are now realizing what an extremely good and decent person David Gower is. Indeed, in the idle hours I spend counting how many clichés Bob Willis can fit into one sentence of his Channel 9 television Test-match commentary, I often wonder how much better David would have fared as captain if he had had the current managerial support group. The combination of manager Peter Lush's public-relations background, his confidence in dealing with the press and (perhaps his greatest asset) his inalienable common sense, together with assistant manager Micky Stewart's reputation as a no-nonsense disciplinarian, removes many extraneous pressures from a captain's shoulders. The skipper is thus left free to devote himself to the job in hand: leading his men on the field. On overseas tours, nowadays, that is more than sufficient. But enough of all that for the moment. Back to a favourite, and exponentially more interesting topic: MOI!

I am finding it very difficult to establish a regular sleeping pattern, since my circadian rhythms would appear to be seriously out of kilter. I assume this is what other folk advert to as jet-lagged. It does not help, sharing a room

with Philippe-Henri Edmonds, whose insomniac idiosyn-
crasies are legendary in the England cricket camp. Four
players have been granted the privilege of a single room
this tour; Mike Gatting (the captain), John Emburey (the
vice-captain), David Gower, in appreciation of his seniority,
and Phil Edmonds, by virtue of the fact that he is such an
impossibly awkward blighter that nobody else will share
with him. His relentless attempts to tune into the BBC's
World Service on the radio are positively Heath Robinson.
Coils of wire, attached to extruded coat hangers, wrapped
around television aerials, affixed with drawing pins to the
ceiling, and festooned across the outside balcony, make the
Edmond's hotel love nest appear more like an electricity
generating station or a nuclear fusion power plant than a
connubial boudoir. He is awake every morning at 5 a.m.,
and orders that Aussie/American favourite, steak and eggs.
Being woken up at 5.15 by some fifteen-stone nutter
watching breakfast TV and eating steak and eggs in bed
beside you certainly adds a completely new dimension to
the phenomenon of morning sickness.

Australian television is dominated to a large extent by
commercial channels. The ABC (the Australian equivalent
of our BBC) would appear to have a hard time competing
with the Murdoch, Packer, Fairfax, Bond, and Holmes à
Court media empires. The copious amount of advertising
is most intrusive for a newcomer. Not only do the channels
devote a lot of time and airspace to advertising products,
but even more energy seems to be devoted to promoting
themselves. Channel 9, Kerry Packer's old outfit, which
generally achieves the top ratings, is a case in point. Most
of the evening news time is devoted to the message that the
news is coming and that it will be absolutely spiffing when
it arrives. Consumers, I believe, should be allowed to make
such quality assessments for themselves, and not have them
gratuitously foisted upon them. Perhaps the marketing
whizzkids are not sufficiently convinced of the value of their
own product. Or maybe this is just the Aussie way. With

luck Alan Bond's buy-out of the Packer TV empire will change matters.

The Aussie way of depicting history, incidentally, is possibly worth a mention. Not that I can blame the Australians for their somewhat distorted account of the infamous 1932–3 'Bodyline' series; all chauvinists play with facts. The Hayes/Schultz film of that name, however, is currently being screened as I write, and although I was not personally doing the rounds in the heyday of Bradman and Jardine, I am nonetheless prepared to take it on higher authority that the entire production bears as much relation to the truth of the matter as Marilyn Monroe's death certificate. There is such a thing, of course, as dramatic licence, but in this case dramatic licence moves into the realms, if not on occasions of invention, then perilously close to fiction. On a purely physical level, for instance, the public-sympathy odds are stacked heavily in Australia's favour from the outset. Australian batsman Don Bradman is tall, dark, seraphically good-looking, with incandescent watery blue eyes and a fair monopoly on righteousness. In truth, Bradman was never more than of very average physical stature, and was to conventional film-star good looks what Robert Redford is to Test cricket. The English, on the other hand, are with few exceptions an irretrievably dastardly bunch. Jardine is depicted as a demonic obsessive, whose ears stick out at forty-five degrees to his head and wiggle satanically as he plots the 'leg-theory' downfall of 'Bradmin' and the entire Australian 'crickit' team. Apparently the real Jardine was an elegant patrician, and by no means the unequivocal bounder and cad he would appear to be in the film. None of this, however, is half as significant as the actual timing of the screening. Old resentments for things which happened over fifty years ago still run deep. Jardine's restricted use of leg-theory, which, compared to the relentlessly murderous assaults of Lillee and Thomson in their heyday, was a positive picnic, continues, nevertheless, to be a controversy which epitomizes the perennial and not always entirely friendly rivalries between the mother country and her former colony. As the 1986–7 'Clashes for the Ashes' begin to warm up it is interesting that certain sectors of the Australian media see fit to remind us that, when all is said and done, all Aussies are fine, bonzer folk, and equally all Pommies are bastards. Come to think of it, one day that might make a good title for a book.

2

The Melbourne Cup

Two consecutive days is quite enough time to devote to any one man. Indeed the World Health Organization would probably rule that anything more than a one-night-per-annum exposure level to the insomniac shenanigans of PHE could seriously damage your health. On the third morning after my arrival in Australia I therefore flew off to Melbourne, while the England team emplaned for Kalgoorlie, materialistic Mecca of gold mines and whorehouses. That disciplinarian, Micky Stewart, would just have to find a way of keeping the boys out of the gold mines. Phil and David Gower, however, elected to make the journey by overnight train. Beefy Botham had implied that he too would like to take the twenty-six-hour train trip, but the management decided otherwise. Twenty-six hours of the irrepressible Beefy in a confined space with gratis booze was not considered to be a terribly good idea.

On the flight from Adelaide to Melbourne I read *Thommo Declares*, the ghosted biography of Jeff Thomson, erstwhile pace bowler, and *enfant terrible* of Australian cricket. I am not too wild about the genre of ghosted biographies. To my lights only people who are dead should invoke the privilege of opting out of the hassle of recounting their own version of events. Unfortunately, with one or two remarkable exceptions (Peter Roebuck, Vic Marks, Mike

Brearley, all Oxbridge men), most cricketers take the easy
option, pick up the loot, and let some other poor bloke do
the graft. Too often the results tend to be of fairly iridescent
mediocrity, with oleaginous sycophancy as the major hallmark. Until such times, however, as cricketers develop the
time, the inclination and sufficient words in their vocabu-
lary to write their own stuff this is the type of sports book
we shall tend to be saddled with.

Thommo's book makes interesting if not consistently
edifying reading. Frequent expletives have patently been
deleted, but there is nonetheless an obvious effort by
biographer John Byrell to promote an uncompromisingly
macho image. The book pays joyous tribute to those quin-
tessential Aussie values of playing cricket, swilling beer,
swearing voraciously, and bonking oneself stupid. 'Ian
Botham', says Thommo, 'would make a great Aussie.' It is
still not known whether Mr Botham will be taking legal
action.

The book continues very much along a the-only-good-
Pommie-is-a-dead-Pommie line. England is dispensed with
as a 'shithole', since there are no beaches to speak of. In
fairness I suppose one has to admit that there are not too
many surfers' paradises in the immediate vicinity of Lord's,
The Oval, Edgbaston, Trent Bridge or Headingley. The
one-time fastest man on earth has a more serious complaint,
however, in that the wild pigs in England 'had all been
cleaned out by something like the fourteenth century'. To
tell the truth, it seems perfectly incredible that someone
who played cricket against England teams until as late as
1985 should have come to the conclusion that the species
has died out *completely*.

Most of this, of course, is designed to reinforce the
received image of the Aussie fast bowler, but it is, in fact,
a far cry from the man himself. Thommo spent a brief
period with my husband's county cricket team, Middlesex,
some five years ago, and far from being a loud-mouthed
lout, everyone found him a most polite and personable
character (for an Australian, that is). In retirement,

Thommo now runs his own landscape gardening company, devotes much time to his favourite hobby of growing orchids, and readily admits that he too is becoming a trifle weary of the well-hyped 'gorilla' image. Sadly, these stereotypes are often the only images of Australia promulgated abroad. Currently being promoted is a huge 'Buy Australian' campaign, and many marketing consultants are trying hard to gainsay the predominantly 'ocker' impression created by such advertisements as Paul Hogan's amusing Foster's Lager series, and the Castlemaine XXXX publicity, which is now taking a very definite turn for the better!

The phenomenal box-office success of the film *Crocodile Dundee*, where Hogan plays a crocodile-hunting, beer-downing rough diamond from the Outback, will do little to help those suave sophisticates of the PR world in their 'Australia-really-is-a-terribly-civilized-place' efforts. For the majority of people who have never actually made it Down Under, the Hogans, the Sir Les Pattersons and the 'Terror Thomkins' represent the stereotype Australian they far prefer to believe in.

The flight from Adelaide to Melbourne does not take long, which is just as well. Neither does Thommo's book. It took nearly as long to read it as it must have done to write it.

The Melbourne Cup, which falls traditionally on the first Tuesday of November, is without doubt the high spot of Melbourne society's social calendar. Imagine Ascot, Wimbledon, Henley and a Royal wedding all rolled into one, and you're beginning to get the idea of the Melbourne Cup. The actual Cup day is a State holiday in Victoria, of which Melbourne is the capital, but Melbourne itself is enveloped in frenzied Cup fever for an entire carnival week. To give you an inkling – over the four days' horse-racing this year (Derby Day, Cup Day, Oaks Day and the Ampole Stakes), over 120 million Australian dollars were wagered. (You may reckon on about two Australian dollars to the pound sterling.) Other items of Melbourne Cup expenditure include twelve million Australian dollars spent on ladies' finery: a more modest $250,000 spent on men's clothing; five million dollars spent on rented marquees, car parks, cocktail and private parties; $250,000 on flowers; and twenty-five million dollars on alcohol (including a hundred thousand cases of champagne). The Melbourne Cup, as they would say in Ireland, is good crack.

I was invited to the Cup by Channel 9 television personality, Mike Willesee. Willesee, who, according to aforementioned Channel, 'almost invented current affairs', is an Australian amalgam of Terry Wogan, David Frost and Sir Robin Day. His early-evening chat show is nearly always top of the ratings and no one really knows whether he is going to be acerbic, sympathetic, relentless or generous. His great specialities are hauling double-talking politicians over the media coals, or extracting uncomfortable facts from shady businessmen, and he is compulsive viewing. His researchers also deploy tireless efforts to net international megastars for the programme, but sometimes even they screw it up. So it was that Phil and I were on the programme.

Our appearance was courtesy of a satellite link-up while we were still in England and it was, by all extremely biased accounts, an entertaining performance. I personally cannot remember; it was very early in the morning. Afterwards Phil raced off to Lord's to meet the 9 a.m. deadline for delivering his contract to the TCCB. One of the strictures of the contract was that players would not be allowed to give radio or television interviews, and so Phil simply signed the contract *after* appearing on *Willesee*. Two weeks later, however, he was severely reprimanded and almost dropped from the tour party for our second Edmonds duo, an interview this time with David Frost on *Wogan*. We did a little double act. According to his contract, Phil was not allowed to talk about the cricket, and so, to circumvent the letter of the law, he pretended telepathically to read my mind. It was a harmless, perfectly puerile piece of fun. Unfortunately the British newspaper the *Sun*, whose adoptive offspring, Ian Botham, had been banned from making a TV appearance, decided that Edmonds should not be allowed to indulge in such flagrant rule-twisting with impunity, and the *Sun* solids hit the fan. Phil was summoned to Lord's to see out-going TCCB secretary, Donald Carr, and incoming TCCB secretary, A. C. Smith.

Phil did his unconvincing best to explain that, being a multi-faceted little person, his Frost interview might well have gone along completely non-cricketing lines. He had, for example, recently been involved in a take-over bid for a public company, Black's Leisure, which had created no mean interest in the financial pages of the press.

'Don't be silly,' argued Smith, irritated. 'The reason they wanted you on the show was because you are a cricketer. They wouldn't have wanted you if you'd been a plumber!'

'No,' agreed Phil. 'If they'd wanted a plumber they'd have asked Gatt . . .' In a previous incarnation, Mike 'Gatt' Gatting had been an apprenticed plumber.

Phil made a full, exhaustive and totally insincere apology, had his wrist slapped, and after detention was allowed home with a bad mark and a reprimand. The schoolroom is no place to be when you are thirty-five years old. I fear Phil is going to find this press and media gag very difficult to countenance over the next four months.

Waiting to meet me at Melbourne airport was Carol Bennetto, of William Heinemann (Australia), the publishers whose occasional aberrations result in the production of books such as this. There is currently plenty of excitement in Heinemann (Australia). Not only do they have Jackie Collins and me to deal with, but Managing Director Sandy Grant is up to his neck in the MI5 twenty-five-thousand-part mini-series.

Everyone, by now, must have heard of former MI5 officer, Peter Wright, and the attempts to publish his controversial memoirs in Australia. Her Britannic Majesty's Government is currently resisting such attempts in the Australian courts, defending the principle that intelligence officers do not publish *unauthorized* memoirs. Since no one in their right civil-service mind is going to authorize memoirs the main import of which is that the British intelligence service leaks like a sieve and that former MI5 chief, the late Sir Roger Hollis, was a Soviet mole, this means that the Peter Wrights of life shall publish no memoirs *at all*. Wright, at present living in Tasmania and in fear of his life, and indeed, presumably, of anything subterranean, grey, pro-Russian and furry, is clearly a significant test case. The issue is causing a furore in Whitehall, in Parliament, where Mrs Thatcher has been subjected to some fierce Opposition questioning, and also here in Australia, at the New South Wales Supreme Court in Sydney.

The British Government has fielded the hitherto inscrutable mandarin, Sir Robert Armstrong, to be its main witness. Sir Robert, Mrs Thatcher's Cabinet Secretary and Security Adviser, is also the United Kingdom's most senior and powerful civil servant, and I have had the odd opportunity to study him from relatively close quarters in the past.

I first became aware of the *éminence grise* behind the governmental throne whilst working as a conference interpreter at the 1984 World Economic Summit held at Lancaster House, in London. He seemed to epitomize that quiet, yet probably ruthless, intelligence and efficiency which so hallmarks the real high-flyers in Whitehall's corridors of power. Two years later, in May 1986, I took the same flight as Sir Robert, and British Foreign Secretary Sir Geoffrey Howe, to the World Economic Summit in Tokyo. Unfortunately, I could not quite establish whether the real-life Sir Humphrey Appleby, and the real-life Jim Hacker, saw the irony of the British Airways choice of in-flight trailer movie. It was *Yes, Minister*.

For the purposes of a tour diary, it may well be that Sir Robert's major claim to fame is his privilege in having attended school with that doyen of English cricket writers, *The Times* correspondent, John 'Wooders' Woodcock. It is, nevertheless, also true that the Cabinet Secretary is generally held, in international diplomatic circles, to be one of the coolest customers ever to don a three-piece pinstriped suit and bowler and brolly. It was therefore all the more flabbergasting when we read here in Australia that Sir Robert had been moved to slug a photographer at Heathrow Airport prior to his departure for Sydney. *Slug a photographer?* Sean Penn, probably. A Frank Sinatra gorilla, perhaps. But the head of the British Civil Service? It seemed as likely as Malcolm Fraser losing his trousers . . .

The saga of the ex-Prime Minister's pants was not, however, to dog my promotional tour steps in Melbourne. My last book, *Another Bloody Tour*, an account of England's disastrous 1986 tour to the West Indies, had just arrived here, and was creating quite a stir. especially amongst the male-chauvinist misogynist journalists who prefer to pontificate about it rather than actually *read* it. I have definitely come to the conclusion, especially in the male-dominated arena of cricket, that it is not *what* you write that certain people object to, but the fact that, *as a woman*, you wrote it *at all*.

The first engagement in Melbourne was an interview with Channel 10's Gordon Elliot, on *Good Morning, Australia*. It is the equivalent of our Breakfast TV, and took place in the open air, outside a large department store, Myer's, in a shopping mall.

'You were awful,' said Phil supportively that night when I phoned him.

The next day the producer rang up, and offered me a contract.

Another guest on *Good Morning, Australia* that day was Melbourne society queen, Lillian Frank. Lillian is a large, extrovert, extremely attractive lady, who goes in for a lot of brilliantly outrageous hats and clothes, and speaks with an indefinable mittel-European accent. I warmed to her immediately. She reminded me of an interpreter friend of mine in Brussels.

I think it was John Dryden who wrote in his poem 'Absalom and Achitophel':

Great wits are sure to madness near allied,
And thin partitions do their bounds divide.

Sadly I cannot check this out as I write. Few of the cricket
correspondents have brought their 'Complete Works of
Dryden' with them. Anyway, this interpreter chum of mine
definitely oscillates in that vague critical zone between
outright genius and downright bonkers. She speaks seven
different languages with absolute fluency, all assimilated,
presumably trans-cutaneously, from her seven different
'husbands', and she too operates in that same sort of
indefinable accent which I find so endearing. I remember
interpreting a long time ago at a Council of Agricultural
Ministers in Brussels – so long ago I think it was even
in the days before Popes were being sponsored by beer
companies – and it was very late at night. It was one of
those annual EEC agricultural price-fixing marathons that
often used to go on for twenty-four hours at a stretch.
(They subsequently became much snappier, when some
Calvinistic Dutch President banned booze from the conference room. Nothing quite focuses the average political mind
like the prospect of an alcohol-free twenty-four-hour agricultural price-fixing session.)

Anyway, the proceedings were moving painfully towards
the usual compromise-style dénouement. At such precarious
junctures, the President-in-Office-of-the-Council generally
clears the room of the inevitable congregation of minor
luminaries, leaving the ministers alone with their senior
advisors (usually the permanent representatives in Brussels)
to wrangle over the last few European currency units.

'Seuls les ministres, et *un* adjoint,' ordered the President,
trying to pare down numbers to an absolute minimum.

'Only the ministers and one . . . only the ministers and
one . . . only the ministers and . . .'

My colleague struggled, exhausted, the accent getting
heavier, to find an acceptable rendition of the word
'adjoint'. These adjoints were, after all, the equivalents of
ambassadors.

'Oh, only the ministers,' she fulminated finally, fed up; 'and one other *creature*.'

I recall Britain's Fred Peart looking decidedly amused, with a proportionately deflated permanent representative by his side.

It is strange, is it not, how in life there are certain quite ridiculous things which condition our reactions. A name, an accent, often an association long since forgotten, will make us like or dislike a person for no other reason. So it was that I took to Lillian as soon as I heard her speak. She invited me to her hair salon in Toorak, that exclusive suburb of Melbourne, where they arranged my perenially defiant hair into a chignon for the Melbourne Cup the next day. I had, of course, to wear my hat. My large Liberty's hatbox, gleaming, like the Assyrians' cohorts, in purple and gold, had created great interest among the British Airways cabin crew on my way over. One of them had even asked to try it on. It looked rather fetching, really, though not quite his style.

My hat was of black silk, and extremely large. When I say large, it probably involved about as much fabric as the average spinnaker on a twelve-metre yacht. It was therefore not entirely felicitous that the day of the Cup there was a strong northerly blowing. When they say a strong northerly in Melbourne, they mean about a Force 10. For most ladies the entire day was therefore spent, as indeed it was for me, with one hand clasped to the head, 'Simon Says' fashion. Such deportment does little for anyone's sartorial style.

Fashions at the Melbourne Cup are nothing if not eclectic. Alongside the ostentatiously expensive designer hats, suits and dresses, there were clearly a few little numbers that had been run up all too hurriedly at home on the Singer. Temperatures soared to thirty-five degrees, and an announcement was made that gentlemen would be permitted to remove their jackets in the members' enclosure. Former Prime Minister Malcolm Fraser was there with his wife, Tamie, but declined the opportunity to mislay any further pieces of apparel. There were, though, a number of young men wearing dinner jackets and no trousers. It was difficult to ascertain whether or not they were making a political point and, if so, which. Some chaps had the temerity to wander around in nappies, although given the 'per capita' paucity of lavatories, this turned out to be one of the day's more sensible ideas. Weaving in and out of the assembled rich was a modern-day Robin Hood, and his Merry-to-the-point-of-positively-stotious men. Fortunately for the assembled plutocrats, the Sherwood Forest socialist philosophy on the redistribution of wealth was not a part of their Melbourne Cup manifesto, and they left everyone more or less in peace.

Yes, it is a peculiarly democratic Australian day out. Plebeians and patricians rub shoulders together amicably. Gentlemen in morning-suit attire sip vintage bubbly in the members' car park, whilst slightly urbanized Crocodile Dundees glug tinnies of XXXX wherever the fancy takes them. Middle-aged matrons, displaying more than the odd dimple of cellulite, waddle around, duck-style, in the simoom conditions, furtively downing snifters from a catholic range of ersatz Australian champagnes. Electric green crimplenes, and incandescent fuschia Trevira permapleats find themselves juxtaposed, unabashed, with *haute couture* Diors, Valentinos, Givenchys and Yves St Laurents. There is room at the Melbourne Cup, as there is in this great Australian nation, for just about everyone.

And indeed just about everyone is there. Everyone who is anyone, at least, and a few more besides who are absolutely no one. Conversation buzzes in the élite members' enclosure. What are the current Mrs Robert Sangster and Mrs Tex Harrison wearing? Who is that splendid lady, a pencil-slim dream in black-and-white crêpe de chine, a hat the shape of a main-sail, tacking indefatigably with the gossip columnists' photographers, and positively slam-dunking the odd television camera crew? Yes, to see the world and by the world be seen – that is the name of the Melbourne socialite game. Reputations for drop-dead chic may be won or lost in the space of an hour. That indefinable *je ne sais quoi*, that ephemeral quality, style, is what the high priestesses at the altar of fashion are all aiming at. Some get there, and others don't quite make it. Indeed, as old Blue Eyes Sinatra could tell you, ladies: before you ransack Figgins Diorama (Melbourne's equivalent to London's New Bond Street, Paris's Avenue Montaigne, and Rome's Via Condotti), 'You've either got or you haven't got style'.

On the other hand, there are of course plenty of folk around who would not know an Emmanuel from a C&A, a Piaget from a Swatch, or a vintage Krug from a Great Western méthode champenoise. These are the nicely balanced people quite simply out for a good time, and quietly settling down to the real business of getting seriously ratted.

It was an unforgettable day, and few of the eighty-seven thousand visitors and Victorians who clicked through the turnstiles at the Flemington racecourse would contradict me. The roses, the pride and joy of the Victorian Racing Club, imbued the intoxicating and intoxicated atmosphere with their heady perfume, and nodded wistfully in the wind as punters lost their shirts in a riot of equine folly. There was no shortage of Rollers, Jags and Mercs in the members' car park, the forum where the true patricians congregate to mount modern-age Bacchanalia with the aid of hamper-laden car boots, and to consult the favoured soothsayer on incontrovertible forecasts for the next race.

During an interview with television and radio personality Don Lane on Radio 2UE, I met the other Society Queen of Melbourne, ex-*Vogue* editor, Sheila Scotter. Sheila is an honorary lady member of the Lord's Taverners, a charitable organization which helps deprived, underprivileged and handicapped children by raising funds for sporting facilities and opportunities. Sheila kindly invited me to lunch the next day, and to the celebratory Boxing-Day breakfast to be held in Melbourne by the Lord's Taverners during the fourth Test. Little did I know that this was to herald quite a close working relationship between the Lord's Taverners and Mrs Frances E . . .

My Heinemann minder, Miss Bennetto, and I ended up, exhausted, as guests in the Laurent Perrier marquee, in the midst of which the latest Rolls-Royce model was parked somewhat incongruously amongst a rage of potted hydrangeas, but by this stage who cared who was sponsoring what? In similar marquees all over Flemington, tables groaned with sizzling prawns, barbecued steaks, crayfish thermidor, multitudes of gaily presented salads, gamuts of French and Australian cheeses and symphonies of calories in variegated puddings.

The Melbourne Cup itself was the fifth race, and not due to start until 2.40 p.m. Having always steadfastly maintained that the only way to watch a game of cricket is through the meniscus of a large gin and tonic, it seemed entirely appropriate to watch the first four races on the marquee's monitors through the evanescent bubbles of our hosts' extremely potable Grand Cuvée. Happy watching strategically placed monitors in the marquees, most people could not be moved.

Excitement mounting, some of us clambered up on top of an outside-broadcasting van to watch the race. Stiletto heels wobbling, skirts in the air, titfers perilously anchored, and hair-dos long since dismantled, now-carefree ladies, oblivious to style, hauled themselves up a very dicky ladder and stared.

It was all over in three minutes, the winner At Talaq, a six-year-old bay stallion, trained by sixty-two-year-old veteran Colin Hayes, and owned by Sheikh Hamdan Bin Rasheed Al Maktoum.

The Sheikh and his three brothers, heirs to Dubai's oil wealth, are dominant figures in international racing. A few years ago they owned no more than a few horses, but now they can boast the world's greatest racing team, based mainly in England. The whole business involves expenditure of about ten million pounds sterling per annum. Even multi-millionaire Robert Sangster, with an impressive one thousand horses in training, is very small horse-flesh potatoes compared to the Maktoum bros.

Sheikh Hamdan, who so hates publicity that he donated a million pounds sterling to Bob Geldof's Live Aid fund with a solemn request to leave him out of the limelight, was unfortunately not in evidence at the winner's ceremony, but watched the day's entertainment via a satellite link-up to Dubai. The doyennes of Melbourne society were most distressed that the one person everybody *so* wanted to meet should be absent from the thrash. Indeed, the exotic good looks and far from unhealthy bank balance of the Emirate Prince have caused quite a rapacious flutter in many an Oz-Sloane bosom. Aspiring gold, or even oil, diggers should beware, however, Islamic strictures allow the Muslim Sheikh up to four wives and forty 'acquaintances'; the name of the Sheikh's victorious stallion, At Talaq, means literally 'I divorce thee'.

We wandered home, Carol and I, about 6 p.m., shoes in hand and utterly banjaxed. I fell asleep on my hotel bed, obliterated by a combination of jet lag, wind burn, and heat stroke. I woke up fourteen hours later, at eight the next morning. That day I was flying to the capital of Western Australia, Perth.

It is difficult for Europeans, inured to flying from one European capital to another in the space of an hour or two, to comprehend the vast expanse that is Australia. The flight from Melbourne to Perth covers over two-and-a-half thousand kilometres, and involves a three-hour time change. The itinerary of this cricket tour is a logistical nightmare, involving as it does over thirty such internal flights within the space of four months. There is a putative reason for this intercontinental tangle of criss-crossed flight paths – the Australian Cricket Board (ACB) maintains that it cannot guarantee two consecutive first-class pitches at any one venue. This means that, instead of playing a State game, immediately followed by a Test match, England are obliged to play, for instance, Western Australia in Perth, and then to fly three-and-a-half thousand kilometres to play the first

Test match in Brisbane. The result is a peripatetic aberration of major proportions. Not only are twenty-odd days completely wasted actually travelling, but each flight means a time change, the inevitable hassle of packing, hanging around an airport, a new hotel bed, and a disrupted sleeping pattern.

A few of the tourists are none too wild about flying, either. Peter Lush, Graham Dilley and, to a lesser extent, Mike Gatting, would certainly not be the first to enlist for the Red Devils. The arrangement also means that, instead of a decent two-week stint anywhere, with a couple of well-earned free days for mental and physical recuperation, the majority of such potential rest days are spent in the unremitting grind of travelling. Add to this a few, indisputably much appreciated by the locals, but nonetheless time-consuming up-country matches in places such as Kalgoorlie, Bundaberg, Lawes and Wudinna, and the result is an undeniably punishing schedule by anybody's standards. Perhaps when correspondents berate the team for apparent lack of interest in practice matches, and indeed for the often patently casual approach manifested even in the State matches, they might do well to ask whether there is not quite simply just far too much cricket on this tour. On top of all that, after a five-Test-match series for the Ashes, interrupted by a one-day challenge, there is another apparently gratuitous if crowd-pullingly lucrative codicil of one-day Internationals to round off proceedings. England's professional cricketers, perhaps more than most, suffer from a surfeit of cricket during the home summer season. What with seven days a week spent on the cricket field, and intervening periods devoted to dicing with death on the motorways, it is hardly surprising that men find it difficult to lift themselves for every game. Sports psychologists would probably argue that it is dangerous if players get into the habit of failing to give anything less than a hundred per cent at all times in terms of effort and commitment. Try telling that to sixteen perpetually semi-jet-lagged touring cricketers.

There is, in any event, a growing school of thought which believes that all this drivel about consecutive first-class wickets is so much bureaucratic nonsense; a school of thought which remains profoundly persuaded that whosoever at Lord's agreed to this itinerary had clearly never clapped eyes on a map of Australia; or perhaps whose greedy, mercenary and blinkered gaze could see no further than the balance sheet.

In this year of 'open secrecy' in Australia and 'could it possibly be true that the MI5 bugged Harold Wilson's government?' in England, it really is time the TCCB and MCC took a leaf out of the New Zealand RFU Council's book and opened their meetings to the media.

3

G'day from WA

Perth, the glorious capital of Western Australia, seemed to have developed substantially since my last visit there some four years ago. The ten-minute trip from the new airport to the Sheraton-Perth Hotel provided ample opportunity to assess the creeping urbanization along the magnificent Swan River, that major of the city's manifold attractions. Highrise office blocks and half-finished hotels now jostle for pre-eminence on the water front. Nothing too excessive, however. There is still no shortage of space for folk in Western Australia.

This is my third trip Down Under. The first, on the 1978/9 England tour, was not a particularly happy experience. Nothing to do with the country, which I thoroughly embraced for its unashamed sybaritic enjoyment of the good life. Apart from South Africa, I had never seen such a generally high quality of life and standard of living. The outdoor existence, the kids on the beach whose physiques bore eloquent testimony to an available abundance of fine agricultural produce, and a definite feeling of physical wellbeing all helped to promote my mental picture of Australia as a land of plenty. No, the problem had nothing to do with the landscape, but with the indelibly black blot on it: Phil.

During the second Test, at Perth, Phil had a minor

contretemps with his Middlesex and England captain, Mike Brearley. When I say a minor contretemps, it was an incident which in terms of fallout did as much for Phil's cricketing career as the Americans did for Hiroshima. The entire episode has had more ink devoted to it than to the individual oscillations in weight of the Princess of Wales and the Duchess of York put together, so I shall spare you the tedious details. Suffice it to say that the two Cambridge graduates almost came to blows, had to be prised apart by Essex's John Lever, and Phil did not play Test cricket again on that tour. In fact, things had reached such a ridiculously low communication ebb by the time I arrived that Brearley was refusing to speak to Phil. As an amateur psychologist, and psychotherapist, Mike no doubt had some profoundly good reason for maintaining this zero-interface situation. Trouble was, Phil could not see it. Neither could he see why Geoff 'Dusty' Miller of Derbyshire (now of Essex) should be given the nod ahead of him. He spent the entire tour positively burning with resentment.

How short a man's memory. Essex paceman Neil 'Fozzie' Foster feels, rightly or wrongly, that he has not been given a fair crack of the whip so far on this tour. He too would prefer to be in the thick of it, performing in the middle, rather than being saddled with a veritable super-abundance of pointless free days. Not all tourists who fail to make the XI react like this. I remember on the 1978/9 tour, it was easily forgivable for believing that the very thought of a Test match might have set a certain pace bowler off into yet another majestic migraine. Not so Fozzie. He is young, he is enthusiastic and he wants to prove himself. Deprived of the opportunity, he is naturally not displaying that cheerful, sunny disposition which so characterized him on his successful 1985 tour of India. Phil has started using his Essex nickname 'Angry' (as in Angry Young Man), patently forgetting that there were very few angrier young men than Philippe-Henri Edmonds on the 1978/9 Brearley tour of Australia.

My second visit was as happy as the first one was miserable. I had been recruited as an interpreter to accompany the President of the European Parliament, Madame Simone Veil, and an inter-parliamentary delegation on a two-week whistle-stop tour throughout the length and breadth of New Zealand and Australia. In New Zealand we were accorded grade A diplomatic status. The New Zealanders, after all, were keen to ensure that they could continue to export at least some radically reduced quotas of lamb and dairy produce to their traditional markets in the United Kingdom. Since accession to the European Communities in 1973, however, Britain had been under constant pressure from her European partners to sever former Commonwealth trading links, and to respect that fundamental tenet of Community Preference. Community Preference is one of the basic principles on which Europe's much criticized Common Agricultural Policy is based. In a nutshell, what it means for countries such as Great Britain is this: forget the fact that you have traded with Commonwealth countries for hundreds of years, and that they have geared their entire economies to your domestic market's likes and dislikes. Forget the fact that one of the immutable beliefs of the French and the Germans is that farmers' incomes (unlike the incomes in any other economic category) shall be guaranteed, even when said farmers produce mountains of foods and lakes of liquids that nobody wants, and that therefore their produce is often more expensive than stuff that has been shipped from the other end of the world. Forget all these things, and whatever the knock-down price on world markets, *always buy European*.

Many British politicians, even pro-Marketeers, still find these rules rather difficult to stomach. The problem is, however, as the Continentals never cease to remind us, that if you join a club, then you play by the rules. The British are used to the concept of clubs, of course, and to public-school ideals of playing by rules. Unfortunately for us, most of the Europeans have developed more advanced ideas on gamesmanship.

Well, before this cricket tour diary starts sounding like

a thesis on the Treaty of Rome, I had better get on with the story. The European delegation was the usual carefully 'de Honte'-balanced mixture of nationalities and political hues. There was a Dutch socialist ornithological environmentalist, pinky-green, I suppose, in the political colour spectrum. He spent a lot of time staring hopefully through binoculars, looking for a lesser-spotted kookaburra, or some such unlikely creature. There was an Italian lady communist, inevitably and quite rightly concerned about equal employment opportunities for women, and Aboriginal land rights. There was an Italian energy expert from the Christian Democratic group (a group which in Italy is neither Christian nor particularly democratic), who was concerned about uranium mining. There was a bright young German concerned about more or less everything under the sun, and a dour old Luxembourger concerned about very little other than accounting creatively for his copious expenses. There was an extremely hard-working woman from the British Labour group, a pro-Marketeer (a species even rarer than the lesser spotted kookaburra, or a Christian and democratic Christian Democrat), and the only one who knew much about sheepmeat and lamb, the entire *raison d'être* for this peripatetic League of Nations' jaunt. There was the President of the European Parliament, French Liberal Simone Veil, once tipped as a possible candidate for the first woman Prime Minister of France, a remarkable character who had suffered the trauma of a Jewish adolescence spent in a Nazi concentration camp, and who still bore the mark of her prisoner's registration number etched indelibly on her arm. And then, of course, there was an English lord, who seemed to know little about anything, but who pontificated with great authority, in an impressive golf-balls-in-the-gob public school accent, on virtually everything. But for the partridge in the pear tree, the seven days of Christmas had nothing on us.

The status accorded to the delegation in Australia was no more than B minus. Whilst the New Zealanders were desperate to woo the Europeans, the Australians were far more aggressive in their trading tactics. 'If you don't buy our agricultural produce,' came the message when we arrived in Canberra, 'then you won't be getting our uranium.'

The Prime Minister of the day could not be located to address us, so his deputy was despatched to do the necessary. He did not appear to be excessively conversant with who all these Europeans were. That was fair enough. They certainly had not the foggiest who he was, either.

'Well,' he rounded off with jovial relief, as soon as it was decent to extricate himself from these multi-lingual oddballs who had come twelve thousand miles to see someone who was out; 'well, I'll see you again soon – at the GATT talks' (nothing to do with England's captain) 'in Geneva.'

The European Parliament does not participate in GATT talks, and neither do its members (apart from visits to the odd numbered bank account) ever go anywhere near Geneva.

This exhausting two-week Australasian mission ended in Perth, in the Sheraton-Perth hotel, to be exact, the very pub we are staying in for the State match against Western Australia. I felt a pang of nostalgia as I walked into the lobby, and thought of my Dutch interpreter colleague, Tineke, and her Paris-based sister, Jeanette, who had suffered that punishing schedule in giddy sorority with me. Other members of the delegation had flown home immediately; we on the contrary elected to stay. After a few days' rest and recuperation in Perth, we would soak up the odd ray on the paradise island of Bali before returning to the miseries of a north-European winter.

We did all the things tourists are supposed to do. We bought opals, which turned out to be twice as expensive as analogous stones readily available at places like Asprey's. We took a boat trip down the river, and we shopped in a rather naff little parade, London Court, where developers have gone to great pains to be wrong in every historical detail. The most glaring anachronism is a replica of Big Ben, carefully juxtaposed with fake black-and-white cement 'shoppes' cavorting as Tudor timber structures. It ranks fairly high on the Richter scale of execrable taste, but, deprived as we had been of consumer opportunities, we enjoyed it nevertheless.

Jeanette, at that time, was in her Céline phase. Every season she decides on a designer, and the entire collection is then duly purchased. This trip she had Céline everything, from her sewing kit to her sunglasses, clothes, shoes, luggage, scarves, accessories, jewellery, everything. She was a symphony in Céline, each item carefully co-ordinated, matched, toned and selected . . . *très quinzième*.

We decided to have dinner at the hotel. It was Saturday night, and patently this Saturday night was the night for the Australian Rules team of some province or other to take their respective sheilas out for a do. Jeanette watched, sartorially startled, as some of the definitely non-*couture* creations wafted past her in the lobby bar . . . the sort of incandescent green crimplenes and electric fuschia Treviras still much in evidence four years later at the Melbourne Cup.

'*Mon Dieu!*' she exclaimed finally, a Parisian resident truly rattled by this insouciant Aussie mix 'n' match, by this generalized *laissez-aller vestimentaire*.

'*Je sais que pas tout le monde peut s'habiller chez Céline, mais entre ça, et ce que je vois là, ma fille, il y a un monde . . . UN MONDE.*' ('I know we can't all dress at Céline, but between Céline and THAT – a world of difference, my dear, a world.')

Despite her initial shock at some of the more casual aspects of Australian life, however, Jeanette fell deeply in love with the place, and comes back to Australia every year on an annual pilgrimage from Paris. Far more sympathetic, perhaps, the laid-back Aussies than the uptight French.

Such were the thoughts of fun times shared, and dear friends sorely missed, as I descended on the Sheraton-Perth hotel. The team arrived a few hours later, having won the rain-affected fixture at Kalgoorlie. A sepia-tinted turn-of-the-century photograph of the Kalgoorlie cricket team shows the umpire carrying a shotgun, an eloquent indication, perhaps, of the type of behaviour prevalent on the field in those days. Civilization, by all acounts, has taken a tighter grip on the place now, and the town council is even trying to clean up the notorious image of the place as a gold-mining town studded with tin-shack whorehouses. Business is apparently still thriving in both fields of activity, and it takes the ladies of the night no more than a year to eighteen months to earn enough loot to up and off on the compulsory overseas tour. The council has currently taken to bulldozing down these rather tacky brothels, though graciously they do forewarn the inmates and their clients. Who knows, otherwise, how many other eminent persons might be inadvertently caught with their pants down? It does seem a shame, though, that such a celebrated tourist attraction should be so summarily flattened . . . sort of thing the old Greater London Council (God rest its soul) would slap a preservation order on . . . probably even give a grant to as well . . .

Phil had been twelfth man for the match, and so had taken the opportunity to visit a gold mine. Well, he would say that, wouldn't he? In fairness, he did bring me back a gold nugget for the much-vaunted wedding anniversary. Nothing to get hysterical about, girls, it was hardly a boulder, but I suppose I can have it made up into something suitably gaudy and crass if we stop off in Hong Kong on our way back. In fact, I am given to believe that Phil actually has some small interest in the open-cast mine he visited. When I say small, it is probably nugatory, but who cares if I have got the one nugget? Anyway, be the interest large or small, I always wanted a husband who owns a gold mine.

Perth, at the moment, is vibrant, seething with excitement over the America's Cup, which is being bitterly contested up the coast in Fremantle. Even those of you who know little of this somewhat esoteric, rich man's sport of twelve-metre yacht racing will nevertheless recall the tremendous national jubilation surrounding Australia's victory over the Americans at Newport in 1983. Self-made Pom-done-good Perth multi-millionaire Alan Bond and the crew of *Australia II* did the impossible in capturing the Auld Mug (as the priceless Garrard's trophy is affectionately called) from the United States, after the Americans' 132-years' dominance in the competition. The Bond syndicate employed genius Ben Lexcen to design the boat, with its radical winged keel, and no expense was spared on sail-makers, sports psychologists, and technical back-up staff in an effort to guarantee success over the man many people still believe to be the best twelve-metre sailor in the world, maestro skipper, Dennis Conner, and his 'Red Boat', *Liberty*.

The story of the commitment, the heartache, the joys and the pains of that epic victory are well documented in the controversial book *Born to Win*, written by, or at least ghost-written for, the *Australia II* skipper, John Bertrand. Bertrand's version of events is not entirely accepted by all parties concerned and is, quite forgivably, a fairly free exercise in self-promotion. It is nevertheless an intriguing insight even for non-aficionados like myself, and the passages on sports psychology make quite revealing reading. It may come as a shock, for example, that Australians, for all their ostentatiously brash, macho and assertive profile, apparently feel themselves deep down to be second best. The 'tall poppy' syndrome predominates in the Australian consciousness – a philosophy which advises: don't be a tall poppy, don't be head and shoulders above the rest; don't strive for excellence: accept the position as second best; remember that the tall poppies are usually the ones that get their heads blown off. On reflection, the Australians are certainly far from being alone in granting this attitude such widespread currency.

Bertrand explains how years of defeat had inured the Australians to *feeling*, and therefore, to *being* inferior to the Americans. From the beginning of the 1983 series, even though the American defender, *Liberty*, was in most conditions nowhere near as fast as *Australia II*, the Australian crew nevertheless had to overcome the psychological disadvantage of *expecting* to be beaten by the Yanks. How Bertrand melded his crew into a galvanized, if not invincible, then at least never-say-die fighting force is perhaps a tract to which losing cricket captains Gatting and Border might usefully devote a few hours' bedtime reading. The fundamental message of the biography is that many people often have to learn to believe in the idea of winning.

The cricket. It does crop up, a tedious leitmotiv in my life, like period pains, hangovers, tax returns and publishing deadlines. But who on earth can be bothered, however, to watch England, in their present state of casual incompetence, playing woeful cricket against a team of virtual teenagers at the WACA (Western Australian Cricket Association), when ten minutes away in Freo (as in Fremantle) the town is knee deep in multi-millionaires? Twelve-metre racing, it is true, is generally perceived as a rich man's sport, but that is not to say that all members of the respective crews are themselves loaded. On the contrary, many yachtsmen will find themselves seriously out of pocket by the end of this Cup series. Although the syndicates either challenging for, or defending, the Auld Mug are positively awash with sponsors' spondulicks, many of the men subjected to the backbreaking effort of sailing the boats are Olympic yachtsmen, and at pains to maintain their amateur status. Indeed, Bertrand even maintains that the day he won the America's Cup he was stony-broke. He resigned immediately, knowing full well that, having reached his personal pinnacle of sporting achievement, there was only one inexorable way to go. He then hired himself a good promotions agent, and is currently commentating on the series for Channel 9 television.

On the free day, Phil and I went off to Freo to visit the British challenger, *White Crusader*. Why on earth the cricket team persists in calling these days 'free' is a mystery to me. The concept of free day would seem to posit an element of work, commitment, sweat and toil on other *de facto* non-free days. Unfortunately, England's performances to date, particularly against Queensland and Western Australia, have been characterized by nothing but the very opposite. There are three minor niggles with the current England touring side, wrote Martin Johnson of the *Independent* newspaper. 'They can't bat, they can't bowl, and they can't field.' It is one of those brilliantly uncompromising one-liners he may have to learn to live with, especially if the tides of cricketing fortune turn. For the sake of historical accuracy, however, it must be admitted that the day Martin penned that obituary, it was all absolutely and incontrovertibly true. Most worrying in the England camp is the continuing lack of form demonstrated by David Gower. In the match against Perth he was dismissed twice without managing to trouble the scoreboard. Ever sympathetic to a man in trauma, the team's in-house sports psychologists have nicknamed the hapless former captain 'Run-Glut'.

Fremantle is a charming little town, some thirty minutes away from Perth on a freeway. It has certainly become a hive of cosmopolitan activity since the thirteen challenging syndicates from six different nations arrived. Apart from the Australian defenders of the Cup, there are challengers from the United Kingdom, Canada, the United States, France and Italy, and each has left its nationalistic imprint on the place. Several syndicates, for example, have constituted their own clubs. The Royal Thames Yacht Club, that is to say, the 1987 British challenger for the America's Cup, has organized for itself and privileged guests a Crusade Club (after the syndicate's yachts *Crusader I* and *Crusader II*). It is a delightfully, terribly, terribly, quintessentially English gentlemen's club, more in place in Pall Mall, London, than Fremantle, Western Australia. Two large, varnished oak doors, a highly polished brass plate discreetly proclaiming its identity and an illuminated bell are its only concessions to ostentation in a row of otherwise nondescript terraced houses. Inside, you could well be on British soil. There is a royal-blue fitted carpet, with an anchor motif, and an abundance of brass and oak. Blazers and cravats seem very much to be the order of the day, although depressed sailors drowning their day's maritime sorrows (on the night we were there it happened to be the badly beaten South Australia syndicate) are permitted less formal attire.

Not all syndicates have set up private clubs, although the ever flash and extrovert Italians lead the field. The Costa Smeralda Yacht Club, Consorzio Azzurra, whose major sponsors include Giovanni Agnelli (he of Fiat fame) and His Highness the Aga Khan, are certainly not to be outdone. The Aga Khan, finding nowhere sufficiently be-Michelin-starred in Fremantle to accommodate his sophisticated billionaire tastes, created his own restaurant, Le Maschere, where the food is as overpriced as it is proportionately underwhelming. He has also renovated, in birthday-cake-icing pinks and whites, an hotel which belongs to his celebrated CIGA chain of expensive watering holes.

There is no shortage of Italians in Australia – indeed after Poms and Greeks they form the largest expatriate population. However, the good burghers of Freo have not taken quite so warmly to the Costa Smeralda super-suave sophisticates as they have to the other Italian contingent, the Italia syndicate. This syndicate is heavily sponsored by Gucci heir, Maurizio Gucci, and is beloved by all for being so totally, utterly and uncompromisingly Italian. During the launch of the syndicate's newest boat, *Italia II*, in La Spezia, for instance, a crane dropped on the multi-million-lira creation and irretrievably sank it. Their spokesman, phlegmatic for anyone under the circumstances, but particularly so for an Italian, a race which, as all we Anglo-Saxons know, is readily given to histrionics and hyperbolics at the merest drop of a capello, commented that the accident had obviously delayed the yacht's development. Sadly, it was never salvaged.

A few weeks later, on a lay day, a few of the crew, dressed up to the nines in all their Gucci-sponsored designer gear, went out sightseeing in their brand new Alfa Romeo sports car. Hurtling around a blind corner, very much *all'italiano*, they ran straight into a huge kangaroo. Leaping out of their somewhat dented vehicle, resplendent in the afternoon sun in their red, white and green yachting uniforms, they were initially horrified at having killed Australia's greatest symbol. But tourists after all are tourists, and Italians after all are Italians, and so they hoisted up the old roo and took a few photographs, posing beside him. One of the culprits even went so far as to dress the demised marsupial in his Via-Condotti-eat-your-heart-out designer jacket. Suddenly, however, the kangaroo, who had only been stunned, came to his senses and hopped off back into the bush, taking with him the Gucci coat, and the driver's licence, credit cards, cheque book, wallet, and car keys. The poor Italians had to hitch a lift back into Freo, trying to explain their hilarious tale in broken English to an incredulous local.

The highly gregarious Italia syndicate has a club as well. It is called Casa Italia, all white, red, green and jolly, and looks like nothing so much as a huge spaghetti parlour. They also have a shop, where pretty girls unable to charm one of the more susceptible crew members may buy their own Gucci T-shirts, sweaters, and down-lined vests. In fact, for a price the entire range is available right down to the Gucci-designer underpants!

We went to visit the British challenge on not, perhaps, the most propitious of days. *White Crusader*'s mast had been badly bent, and the race had inevitably been lost. Shore manager Andrew 'Spud' Spedding, whom Phil and I have known over some four years, was nevertheless in good spirits and generally pleased with the way things were shaping up. We had met Spud, along with mutual friends, in a pub in Devon during the 1983 America's Cup in Newport. He had just parted company, not entirely amicably, with Peter de Savary, the leading sponsorship light in that particular failed British effort. Current *White Crusader* skipper, Harold Cudmore, had also resigned, unable to take any more of de Savary's unsavoury philosophy of creative tension, i.e. not telling people what they were doing the next day, or indeed whether or not they even had a job, in perverse efforts to keep them on their toes. This British challenge has certainly rid itself of individual and dominant patriarchs, a common enough feature in yacht racing, and is managing itself as a listed company along Business Expansion Scheme lines.

Yes, indeed, times have certainly changed since the days of Sir Thomas Lipton, that Grand Old Man of America's Cup challengers. Sir Thomas was denied membership of Britain's Royal Yacht Squadron until he was virtually dead, because he was 'in trade', a cardinal sin for those ever-so-amateur chaps running things in Cowes in the 1920s and 1930s. Although 'Sir Tea', as he was affectionately known, never directly used any one of his five Cup challengers to promote his product (they were all named 'Shamrock' . . . Heaven knows what riot the marketing boys would have today, with combined concepts of 'Cup and Tea' to work on), it was nevertheless obvious that his involvement in these competitions did his corporate profits no harm whatsoever.

It is therefore more than passingly ironic that it is none other than the British themselves, those watchdogs of the 'play up, play up, and play the game' Corinthian ethic, who have used their best endeavours to allow the trade in on the twelve-metre act and all that that signifies in terms of creeping commercialism. Initiatives have been implemented to do away with Rule Twenty-six of the Cup, the last barrier to overt sponsorship/public relations packages. The British challenge, relatively impecunious compared to many of the syndicates in Freo, was obliged to accept over a million pounds from the manufacturers of White Horse Whisky for changing their boat's name from *Crusader* to *White Crusader*. Nothing too offensive, really, and certainly not half as provocative as the *Société des Régates Rochelaises*, whose challenge is heavily sponsored by a French photographic company, Kis France. They have named their boat *French Kiss*, and during press conferences their skipper, Marc

Pajot, talks in delightful *double entendre* Inspector Clouseau-genre English about improving our *French Kiss* techniques.

The British, of course, do not want anything even half so vaguely vulgar and nasty. Perhaps a nice, inoffensive, generic word such as 'White' incorporated into the boat's name, discreet sponsors' logos on the spinnakers, but nothing in any way crass or flashy on the mainsails or headsails. It remains to be seen whether sponsors, whose financial commitments run into millions of pounds, will be satisfied with that. At all events, a life-sized white horse adorns the British challenger's yard, and the gaily painted sheds pay ample tribute to another red, white and blue sponsor, British Airways.

It is difficult to know what, besides the Peter de Savarys of life, could ruffle Spud Spedding. The bent mast had cost *White Crusader* her hard-earned third position in the challenger series, but slots in the table tend to change on a daily basis, and Spud, for one, was not going to spend the rest of the day crying over a spilt mainsail. As we waited for the disabled yacht to be towed in, he regaled us with even more stories about the wild and wonderful Italia syndicate.

'They are a delight to sail against,' exuded Spud. 'They never want to do too much work on deck in case they mess up their natty uniforms. And we know when they're about to tack. They all take one last, final drag, and throw their cigarettes overboard.'

Despite funds of around five million pounds to draw on, the Royal Thames Yacht Club's *White Crusader* and her entourage are still very poor relations compared to the New York Yacht Club and *America II*, the Royal Perth Yacht Club with the affluent Bond and Kookaburra syndicates, and the astoundingly successful Royal New Zealand Yacht Squadron with the brilliant young skipper, Chris Dickson, and her Kiwis *KZ-3*, *KZ-5*, *KZ-7*. Where other crews might rest after sailing, the *White Crusader* team is often obliged to compensate for the relative paucity of back-up staff by helping out on shore afterwards, hauling sails and swabbing-down decks. Sailing twelve-metre yachts is a round-the-clock operation, and I saw Phil blanch visibly as he heard of the British crew's normal daily schedule: up at six; breakfast; weight training; jogging; heave the heavy sails on board; sail for three, four or five hours, often in that monstrously strong, yet for landlubbers wonderfully refreshing, wind the locals call the Fremantle Doctor; haul the far heavier wet sails off the yacht; lay them out to dry; scrub down the deck and start doing odd jobs in the yard; perhaps a run; dinner; collapse. And all this, in the case of many of the crew, for nothing more than their board and keep, and the sheer joy of the sport. Perhaps Phil's mind turned to certain putatively professional cricketers, pulling in five- or even six-figure sums, and hysterical at the *slightest* suggestion of an extra net, ten minutes' desultory fielding practice, or the very idea of belittling themselves sufficiently to make *deus ex machina* appearances in between Test and State games. True sport, I'm sure, can only ever be amateur. Budgetary restrictions being what they are, the British challenge does not have available cash for expensive trendy extras. Sport psychologists count as such and so Cudmore and Spedding thought it only fair to lift a few ideas from the crews of their rivals.

'And by the way, no sex,' suggested Spud one morning, almost subliminally, in his early-morning team talk; 'absolutely no sex during the elimination rounds.'

The stunned silence was finally broken by one all-macho winch-grinder. If normal conjugal relations were to be banned, he threatened, then he, for one, would just have to take matters into his own hands, behind the back of the sail shed.

We could have stayed all day with Spud, listening to tales of alchoholic admirals, outrageously rude commodores, and unstoppable yachting bores.

My favourite Spud story is about the lord, who, having heard similes about a man of his station, duly proceeded to get as drunk as one. It was in the hey-day of those majestic vessels, the J-boats, and his Lordship, in a fairly plastered condition, fell asleep below deck one evening, and awoke to find the ship once again at sea.

'Would you care to take the helm, my Lord?' asked the captain, with due deference, when his Lordship emerged finally.

'No thank you, Smithers,' replied his Lordship blearily; 'I never touch a thing before breakfast.'

Or perhaps the other tale, which Spud tells in his own inimitable fashion, about the Algernon Cleft-Palate-Smythe-type yachting bore, who collared the retired Admiral in the Royal Thames Yacht Club, and insisted on regaling him with the tedious minutiae of some competition he had once been involved in.

'And it was probably the Wednesday, no there again it might have been the Thursday, because on the Wednesday it was the ebb tide and then on the Thursday we had the flow tide . . . no there again it was my wife's sister's birthday on the Tuesday, I remember because we took her out to Claridges, and the day after we had the flow tide . . . and there we were sailing to leeward . . . no there again we must have been sailing to weather . . . because I remember saying to old Buffy . . . I remember saying, "Buffy, old man, Buffy, there's only one way to sail this boat, and that's to weather," . . . and Buffy said to me . . .'

The epic non-drama dragged on for a further ten minutes, as the Admiral's far-away look became progressively further and further away. Finally, he had had enough.

'Carruthers,' he shouted, summoning one of the discreet and impeccably dressed, stony-faced flunkies whose mission it was to emerge magically from the Club's gin-and-tonic mists whenever needed. 'Carruthers, come over here like a good man, and listen to the rest of this fellow's story for me.'

We left Spud and the British challenge to deal with the bent mast, and returned to Perth for Phil's team meeting. Unfortunately, listening to Spud's tales of sailing folklore, I had omitted to ask him the one question that had been preying most on my mind. What was actually meant by a twelve-metre yacht?

'It's odd,' I mused to Phil. 'I had always assumed it meant the length of the boat, but now I've just read that Bondy's victorious *Australia II* measured 64 feet 7 inches, which makes it twice as long as twelve metres.'

'Really!' exclaimed Phil impatiently, in that same please-don't-ever-mention-the-subject-to-me-again voice with which he quashed my embryonic, 'why-don't-left-arm-round-the-wicket-bowlers-bowl-*at*-the-wicket-rather-than-*round*-it?' interest in cricket. 'How can you be so totally stupid? *Everybody* knows twelve metres refers to the height of the mast . . .'

Therein lies the fundamental difference between Edmonds P. H. and Edmonds F. E. . . . Whereas I am occasionally bright enough to recognize that I don't know things, Phil is invariably dumb enough to assume he always does. I eventually found the answer to my question from the veteran Perth sailmaker and celebrated round-the-world-yachtsman, Rolly Tasker. Twelve-metre-class yachts, it would appear, are required to comply with the Rating Rule and Measurement Instructions of the International Twelve-metre Class, issued by the authority of the International Yacht Racing Union, in March 1985. The Twelve-metre Class of yacht is based on a complicated quotient, the import of which only Einsteins, giga-byte computers, Mensa folk, and Ben Lexcen intellects of life can fully comprehend. The formula of the equation, for those addicted to the new Fremantle variation of Billionaires' Trival Pursuit, is simply this:

$$R = \frac{L + 2d - F + SA}{2.37}$$

R = Rating (12 metres in this class)

L = Length of the hull measured approximately 180 mm above the waterline. Corrections for girth are applied to this measurement.

d =   The chain girth deducted from the skin girth. The skin girth is measured on the surface of the hull from the deck to a point on the keel about midships. The chain girth (measured at the same place) is the length of line stretched taut from the deck to the same point on the keel.

F =   Freeboard, or height of the hull above waterline.

SA =   Sail area includes the mainsail and the fore triangle bounded by the mast, forestay and deck.

2.37 = Mathematical constant.

Good! Now the semantic nebulosity of twelve-metre has been sorted out, we can all forget it. I merely adverted to the formula because it epitomizes the complicated morass of rules, regulations, practices, and traditions which govern the America's Cup. Many syndicates even have rules experts in their camps to advise them on procedure. During the 1983 Cup, for example, the New York Yacht Club challenged the legitimacy of *Australia II*'s radical winged keel. The NYYC lost its appeal, and simultaneously with it waves of grass-roots sympathy – if we may mix the maritime with the pastoral. Since the New Zealanders in Freo are doing so remarkably well in the 1986–7 Louis Vuitton Cup (the award for the successful challenger who will subsequently meet the successful defender), there is currently more American hoo-ha about the Kiwis' fibreglass twelves, the 'plastic fantastics' as they have been so appositely nicknamed. *Stars and Stripes* skipper Dennis Conner has all but called the use of fibreglass instead of aluminium cheating, and fellow Californian *USA II* skipper, Tom Blackaller, has been heard to utter similar, if less directly litigious, comments.

No one, as yet, has had the temerity to lodge an official complaint. The New Zealanders have Lloyds, public sympathy, and a lot of brilliant sailing on their side.

Insufficient knowledge of the rules has also led to certain misunderstandings over sponsorship. There are four

Australian syndicates fighting it out for the honour of defending the Cup: two Perth-based syndicates, the Bond syndicate (with its *Australias*), and the Kevin Parry-led Taskforce syndicate (with its *Kookaburras*), which is presently leading the field. There is also a South Australia syndicate and an Eastern Australia Defence syndicate, with its rhyming slang yacht *Steak 'n' Kidney*, so christened to rhyme with Sydney. Over-enthusiastic donors in the latter two syndicates had not all realized, however, that no matter which Australian syndicate were to win the Cup, that delightfully redundant Garrard artefact would continue to remain bolted securely in place at the Royal Perth Yacht Club. The competition is not between countries or cities, but between individual yacht clubs, and the Australian syndicate which wins the right to defend the Cup, irrespective of whence it comes, will do so on behalf of the Royal Perth Yacht Club.

This apparently came as something of a shock to certain Sydney hot-shot punters, who had fancied the idea of the next series being battled out under the shadow of the Opera House and the Harbour Bridge. There seems a degree of poetic justice, however, in the fact that the Western Australian underdogs who wrested the Auld Mug from the New York Yacht Club, a club dominant for a 132 years in the sport, should be allowed to cherish it while it still remains on Australian soil. Distressingly, though, looking at the Kiwis and the ravening Yanks, that may not be for very much longer.

The Government of Western Australia, expecting vast profits from the tourist industry, has also ploughed millions of dollars into the Cup and its peripherals. Like Treasurer Paul Keating's tax returns, however, the massive influx of tourists has failed to materialize. Neither does a sudden flood of twelve-metre aficionados seem likely to develop at this late stage to amortize capital investment. The press and syndicate circuses are already *in situ*, and locals fear that there could be even heavier losses if the Americans do not make it through to the finals. Nevertheless, there is no underestimating the groundswell of nationalism, even chauvinism, generated by winning at sport, be it never so exotic a sport as twelve-metre racing. Stickers, posters, advertisements, jingles, lapel badges, T-shirts, you name it, everything here in Perth proclaims, 'G'day from WA'. Eileen, the wife of entrepreneur Alan Bond (who has probably done as much as any one man to put Western Australia on the map) is playing a protagonist's role in this State promotion. It is tragic, however, that so few Eastern Australians, because of the vast distances involved, and the exorbitant price of internal flights compared to cheap, bucket-shop international fares, ever even visit the place. After Sydney, Perth must surely rate as the most beautiful of Australia's state capitals. The second Test in Perth stands out like a beacon in a rather gloomy early itinerary. If nothing else it means another trip to Freo, which is presently so full of sailors. And I am a nice girl.

It has become irritatingly necessary to go to WACA and watch some cricket. Being a Roman Catholic (although ever so slightly lapsed, due to theological difficulties in swallowing the encyclical De Humanae Vitae hook, line, and *ex cathedra* sinker), I always feel obliged to do some penance after having some fun. Penance! Torquemada in the worst excesses of the Spanish Inquisition would never have inflicted this on the worst religious deviant. The cricket was worse than grotesquely bad, which I can often prove acceptably amusing. It was just inadequately shambolic, which at best is intensely embarrassing. The Australian press corps was feeling mightily chuffed, and offering generous odds on England's patently inexorable annihilation at the first Test in Brisbane. In Western Australia's second innings England dropped at least seven dolly catches. I say 'at least' because there could have been plenty more and I may have missed some. My eye-surgeon brother, Brendan, currently devoting himself to being a little bannister on the stairway of life, researching into sickle cell anaemia in Jamaica, discovered when I was out there, on England's last disastrous tour, that I could hardly see.

Not that there is anything I want to do to rectify this highly satisfactory state of affairs. I do not want to end up with vision so perfect that I am given incontrovertibly empirical evidence of something which I have vaguely suspected for some time now: that I have spent the last four or five years sleeping with a big, bald, fat man.

On the evidence of that day's cricket, at least, Johnson of the *Independent* was perfectly right. England could not bat, they could not bowl and they could not field.

Watching as they dropped the seventh easy catch, people wondered seriously whether the England team was capable of catching the next morning's plane to Brisbane.

4

Brisbane: some cricket, at last

The flight from Perth to Brisbane, traversing the entire continent of Australia, involved about seven hours' travelling, a three-hour time difference, and a stop-over to change planes in Sydney. It was perhaps not entirely fortunate that those of our merry band who need their regular fix of tabloid twaddle raced off to buy the local evening paper. Oh, dear! It was the same phenomenon that reared its ugly head in Trinidad last year and caused so much trouble. Old-guard British correspondents often erroneously assume that the copy they file back home to London will be read at breakfast-time, forgotten by lunchtime, and consigned to the immortality it deserves, as people's fish and chip wrappings, by tea-time. How they underestimate the wonders of modern technology! Nowadays a piece written in Australia and filed to London may well be winging its way back within hours, boomerang-style, to knock its originator on the head. In fairness, it must be granted that this 'talk back' school of reporting often lifts chunks out of context, usually the most controversial and scurrilous chunks, and does a cut-and-paste job that is ideally designed to precipitate intercontinental aggro of mega-proportions.

The London *Evening Standard*'s cricket correspondent, John Thicknesse, had apparently filed a piece on the Somerset County Cricket Club's ritual blood-letting. The

Somerset committee, for a variety of reasons (many of which will probably never be fully comprehended unless or until captain Peter Roebuck releases his own deeply disturbing chronicle of events), decided to dispense with the services of West Indians Viv Richards and Joel Garner, and to enlist the services of New Zealander Martin Crowe instead. Far be it from me, a mere woman, to involve myself in the purely cricketing rationale of this move. Indisputably, Viv Richards is one of the world's finest batsmen, and Joel Garner still a splendid fast bowler. The fact remains, nevertheless, that despite the presence of these two West Indians and Ian Botham, the Somerset team has been doing very poorly. There is talk that the triumvirate of superstars was a clique within the dressing-room, and an influence in many ways deleterious to young, suggestible county players. Lest I start involving Heinemann in yet another mammoth legal battle, however, suffice it to say that one fact remains beyond the shadow of a doubt. Superstars who may well perform miracles to packed crowds in the international arena are not necessarily as liable to give their all on a wet Sunday afternoon playing Glamorgan at Swansea. I rest my case, and await with interest the evidence of my learned Cambridge legal colleague, Mr Roebuck.

Botham, upon hearing of his two mates' dismissal, immediately tendered his resignation to boot. This was perceived by many of the public to be a loyal and generous course of action. Considering that the Somerset committee had stood by Botham while he was suspended for nearly an entire season for drugs offences, it is perhaps difficult to decide where primary loyalty should lie. Whatever the merits of the case, supporters' groupings were quickly mustered on both sides, and the resultant civil war made the Yorkshire County Cricket Club/Boycott issue look like a High Commission cocktail party. The internecine strife has become so ugly that in a press conference here in Australia Botham has warned Roebuck (who will be arriving in Brisbane to cover the tour for the *Sunday Times* of London, and the *Sydney Morning Herald*) that he would be safer staying at home. Phil says that kind of totally unveiled threat is all 'piss in the wind' (I've noticed, incidentally how the level of Phil's concepts, conversation and metaphors plummets when he has spent more than two weeks in the egregious intellectual company of a touring team), but I am not so sure. Peter would probably, in any event, be well advised to give Botham a very wide berth. Since childhood I have always been physically frightened of people whose bodyweight in kilos is numerically higher than their IQ.

In his place Thicknesse had branded Botham a boorish bully, which is about as original an observation as roses are red, violets are blue, sugar is sweet and Mike Gatting likes cheese and pickle sandwiches. It was, if I am not much mistaken, virtually the same expression used by the *Mail*'s brilliant roving, award-winning correspondent, Ian Wooldridge, and by Phil's biographer and *The Times* correspondent, Simon Barnes, in Trinidad last year, and the consequent eruptions were not dissimilar. On this occasion it was not Botham's ghost-writer from the *Sun* who showed him the ex-libris Thicknesse snippets. For it often seems that some reporters deliberately goad the mercurial Beefy into doing things, saying things, and over-reacting to things in order to provide good tabloid copy. This time it must have been some other either deliberately malevolent or inadvertently thoughtless cog in the cricketing circus wheel. Botham duly exploded into a suitably Olympian rage, only the calming influence of managerial proximity preventing Thicknesse's comments from becoming self-fulfilling prophecy. Botham turned to two of the England team's younger acquisitions, and told them, although not perhaps in so felicitously turned a phrase, that they would rue the day should he ever catch either of them talking to Thicknesse.

The fact that the pair of them spend their travelling time with their Walkmans clapped uncommunicatively on their heads, the one of them obliged to down innumerable tinnies of Fosters in an effort to dispel his fear of flying, and the other unlikely to recognize Thicknesse even if he were to walk around clad in nothing but plastic laminated copies of the *Evening Standard*, rendered the Botham diktat somewhat superfluous. Nevertheless, certain members of Botham's vicariously aggrieved cohorts went so far as to suggest that captain Mike Gatting should be enjoined to stop playing cards with said sacrilegious correspondent. Neither must anyone have a drink with him in the bar . . . or share their sandwiches with him . . . or play him at conkers . . . or let him look at their hamster . . .

This was my first visit to Brisbane, but Queensland's reputation had preceded it. When I first arrived in Australia, opinion polls had been suggesting that the State's incumbent Premier, Nationalist Sir Johannes Bjelke-Petersen, was no longer the leader whom the majority of Queenslanders wanted. Sir Johannes has held the reins of power in this State for almost twenty years, and the opinion polls were sort of right. Sixty-one per cent of the electorate did *not* support the continued leadership of this arch-conservative (for want of a more right-wing expression) politician. Thanks, however, to a gerrymander system that would disgrace most regimes with vague pretensions of democracy, Sir Joh was returned to office with an overall majority, on the basis of a mere thirty-nine per cent of the vote. The politics here are frankly scandalous, and what is worse is that everybody knows it. Any reform of this patently unjust and rather selective electoral system would have to be effected at Federal level, however, and Queensland represents a can of constitutional worms that the increasingly less popular Prime Minister, Bob Hawke, is unwilling to open.

He could well have done so many things, Labor Prime Minister Hawke, when first he ascended to power in 1983. A poll taken at the time indicated that more Australians believed in Bob Hawke than believed in God. There would be no point, of course, conducting a similar poll on Margaret Thatcher in the United Kingdom as the two deities have become virtually indivisible, but certainly

Hawke, at that juncture, could have moved political mountains. He could easily, for example, have enacted legislation to settle the vexed issue of Aboriginal land rights, a shameful running sore that continues to scar Australian society and history, and a problem long overdue in its resolution. He could, in all probability, have addressed the canker of the Queensland gerrymander, and so very much more. A charismatic character in the inalienably Aussie mould, Hawke had the reputation for being a hard-drinking, sports-loving, ladies' man. His official biographer, Blanche d'Alpuget, does well to encapsulate the carefree charm and the winning ways of the man who once was indisputably Australia's all-time most popular politician.

It is most distressing, therefore, for most people concerned that Mr Hawke has consigned his wayward roué days to the history and biography books, and with them the essence of his charm and charisma. Cartoonists, political analysts, lobby columnists and gossip diarists are distraught at Bob's new holier-than-thou image. No booze, no smokes, on the golf course at some ungodly hour in the morning, as fit as a fiddle, and by all accounts as interesting in inverse proportion. It is therefore with impunity that Sir Joh, not a man to brook external interference, especially not from foreign powers such as Canberra, continues his fiercely independent premiership on the basis of thirty-nine per cent of the vote. In a state such as this, wrote Matthew Engel of the *Guardian*, you might be forgiven for assuming that the team who got fewest runs would win the Test match.

What a glaring lacuna! Four chapters on, and this is the first mention of my favourite cricket correspondent, Matthew Engel. We had, in fact, met up in Melbourne, the evening prior to the Melbourne Cup, where I had subjected the poor boy to the Edmonds' patented remedy for the foolproof cure of jet lag. This remedy involves the indiscriminate ingestion of lots and lots of the old bubbly stuff, and any residual jet lag is forgotten in the onset of the most intergalactic hangover. It is predicated on the ancient train-in-the-tunnel theory, the theory on which acupuncture is based. On the single-track railway line, for instance, only one train can go through the tunnel at any one time. Similarly with the nervous system: nerves can only deal with one message at a time, and therefore a small pinprick may deflect a patient's attention away from a far more excruciating pain. If this all sounds like the most unutterable balderdash to you, you could be right. But I had somehow to convince old Engel that the next bottle would definitely dispel his jet lag. He had just arrived from America, where he was apparently hoping to return to watch the Superbowl in three weeks. I do not know whether it was his speech or my hearing which was by this stage slurred, but for some hours I laboured under the impression that he had every intention of returning to watch a soup bowl for three weeks. Three weeks watching a soup bowl . . . my mind wandered in and out of the bubbles of our eminently potable Great Western méthode champenoise tipple – no wonder *Grauniad* readers have the reputation for being alternative.

'Good night, Matthew,' I said finally, in a garbled valediction, the verbal equivalent of a normal page of *Grauniad* typesetting. 'I'll see you tomorrow at the Cup.' See him tomorrow at the Cup! There would only be Engel and eighty-six thousand and nine hundred and ninety-nine others.

Here we all are, then, three weeks later, on the eve of the first Test, in the land of Sir Joh Bjelke-Petersen, the man who has done for political enlightenment what Colonel Gadaffi has done for international air safety. We were accommodated in the Brisbane Crest Hotel, a friendly enough establishment, where the famous Queensland shellfish is as good as any in the world. The tour has been fairly low-key so far, unlike the last 'Bloody Tour'. No sex, drugs or rock 'n' roll allegations. In fact, the only incident so far has been created by members of the press themselves, which is precisely why you have never read about it.

Law and order, as with all right-wing governments, is a big issue in Queensland. Before we venture any further, it is perhaps worthwhile at this point defining our political terms. Party labels applied in one country do not necessarily imply the philosophies, traditions and beliefs of an homonymous party in another. In Australia, Labor is more or less like our old-style Labour (i.e., without the lunatic fringe, Militant Tendency, effulgent red Trotskyite, equal-rights-for-gay-whales, power-to-the-one-parent-handicapped-lesbian-AIDS-victim curlicues). Liberal, in Australia as in the Federal Republic of Germany, is right-wing conservative (with a big C or a small c, depending on the individual). And Nationalist (as in Sir Joh), is so far to the right that it is almost off the Australian continental shelf and away into the Pacific. Quite apart from these wretched Aussies confounding us poor Poms with their gratuitously misleading political nomenclature, the wags befuddle us even further by cracking jokes about Labor's Bob Hawke turning out to be Australia's most Liberal Prime Minister. Honestly! Centuries-old sacrosanct, socio-political categorizations should not be bandied around like this.

But to return to the law-and-order issue, Phil and I. both stultified by the relentless tedium of the generalized good behaviour on this tour, were delighted to return to the hotel one evening to see a gaggle of pressmen in conclave with the hotel management. It may well be that gaggle is not the most apposite collective noun for pressmen. Gaggle implies geese, and geese implies audible noise, and that is arguably *not* the characteristic most evinced by the press corps. Their mission is to listen to and to watch others, not to constitute the focus of attention themselves. This is an attribute I have not yet managed to assimilate, and it has been remarked that the decibel level in the press box increases exponentially when the one female correspondent, F. E. Edmonds, is in the vicinity. For want of a better word and a Roget's Thesaurus, however, this gaggle of pressmen seemed to be involved in extremely animated conversation with some inordinately irate members of the hotel's management.

Smelling a good story, I immediately produced my Filofax and my *Must de Cartier* fountain-pen. Don't imagine for a moment that we women can't be as competent super-sleuths as the men. Unfortunately, the Filofax was full of good shopping addresses in Sydney, Christmas-card lists, and conversion charts to translate European shoe and clothes sizes into the correct Australian calibration, and the *Must de Cartier* fountain-pen, on the other hand, staunchly refused to flow, and it looks like Melbourne will be the first place to provide replacement refills for the desiccated, burgundy-coloured ink cartridge. Do you suppose this ever happens to Woodcock or Wooldridge?

Unchronicled though it was, this story might well have ended in tears, if not in far worse, had it not been for the fortuitous intervention of the *Mail*'s Peter Smith et al. Peter is very much the *pater familias* of the British press corps on tour, and looks after us all in a tirelessly good-humoured and avuncular fashion. Transport arrangements to and from the airport, collection and delivery of baggage, accreditation and invitations are all taken care of by the unrufflable Smith, who somehow also manages to find time to ghost Geoff Boycott's column and Mike Gatting's latest epic. On the Australian side, Mike Coward of the *Sydney Morning Herald* plays a similar lead role in the Cricket Media Association, and it would be difficult sufficiently to express my gratitude for the many kindnesses these two doyens of the art have bestowed on me on this tour. Anticipating, perhaps not entirely unjustifiably, an avalanche of male chauvinism, and a fair dose of inbred misogynism in Australian cricketing press circles, I could not have been more agreeably surprised. Oh, there have been one or two incidents, but in truth the overwhelming majority of correspondents have been helpful and accommodating. I like to believe that this is for reasons of my own ineffably charming self, but Phil, more objective, maintains it is merely because they know that I am liable to dig the vitriol-tipped stiletto in as deep as any when aggravated.

Martin Johnson of the *Independent* was also very aggravated. Truth to tell, he had been assaultingly aggravated and aggravatingly assaulted by three of the hotel's law-and-order enforcement heavies. It had all started in the bar, when Martin had been involved in a perfectly comprehensible misunderstanding with the Assistant Beverages Manager. Despite the implications of such an onerous title, said Assistant Beverages Manager could not manage to assist young Johnson in the acquisition of any beverage, especially not one of the hop-based variety. Words were exchanged, apparently the only transaction the Assistant Beverages Manager was prepared to enter into with this new arrival to the English cricket press corps, and the next thing he knew, the *Independent* correspondent was being strangle-held/frog-marched out of the establishment in a manner which belied his autonomous status.

It was fortunate that a few by-standing England cricketers were around to witness proceedings, though proportionately unfortunate that they did not have access to a national daily newspaper to relate them. By the time these gorillas had dragged him of 'can't bat, can't bowl and can't field' notoriety out of the hotel, it was alarmingly apparent that he in turn 'could not talk, could not breathe, and could not escape'. With the speed of an 'England cricketer in cocaine-snorting scandal' facsimile, a caucus of press musketeers was quickly mustered to release poor Johnson from the decidedly unslippery grip of these Queensland 'banana benders', and to remonstrate about the United Nations Declaration on Human Rights, Civil Liberties, the Freedom of the Press, in general, and of Martin Johnson, in particular.

It is highly doubtful whether United Nations Declarations on anything have ever percolated quite as far east as Queensland. Certainly, even a cursory glance at the abominable sequence of legislation on Aborigines in this State might lead one to believe that Human Rights were equally as important as Mr Johnson's rights to a well-earned pint at the end of a busy day. I subsequently made three vain attempts to speak to the manager about this needless over-reaction; the first in my own name, the second purporting to come from *Egon Ronay*, and the third as a camouflaged emissary from the *Michelin Guide*. There was no explanation, but in a state such as Queensland, where a doubtfully benevolent but apparently autocratic Premier such as Sir Joh holds sway, I decided that discretion was the better part of valour, and let the matter rest. Johnson, happy to relate, lived to tell the tale, but we had all learned a salutary lesson from the hotel, and after that few people ever shouted loudly for service. Too bad that Martin of all people had borne the brunt of this rather precipitate and boorish behaviour. He is a young, bright, intelligent and dry-humoured addition to the tour, and it is easy to think of at least a dozen characters those goons could more rightfully have picked on. As it was, the whole fiasco reminded me forcibly of the wild hyperbole so prevalent in the maddest over-the-top-excesses of a Tom Sharpe novel.

Talking about OTT excesses, the Premier himself, the doughty Sir Joh, is as close as makes no matter to a real-life Tom Sharpe character. Joh-ologists suggest that he has almost become a self-parody, imitating himself in a sort of vaudeville amalgam of cracked metaphors and off-the-cuff comedy. He talks in deprecating terms about his political opponents, the Labor party – 'the old guard, the new guard, the mud guard' . . . it is all fairly unsophisticated slapstick comedy stuff. He affects to forget who people are when addressing or introducing them . . . 'well, it doesn't matter, does it? You know who you are yourselves.' And, less appealingly, he is totally dismissive of anyone who disagrees with him. He would not appear to be the sort of politician interested in rigorous debate or informed argument, but rather someone who is utterly convinced that he is right, and that anyone who dares to contradict him is a treacherous nincompoop. His highly controversial personality has spawned a flock of imitators. the leading exponent of whom is a conservatory-trained pianist and Jesuit seminarian, Gerry Connolly. Certainly, watching the real article at work during television interviews put me in mind of a variation on one of the many brilliant one-liners from the uncannily prophetic play *Pravda:* 'Mickey Mouse, you might be inclined to believe, wears a Sir Joh Bjelke-Petersen watch.'

It is all the more amazing, therefore, in a state which by most outsiders would definitely be considered one of the last bastions of male chauvinism, that the Lord Mayor of the capital city, Brisbane, should be, of all things, *a woman*. Liberal alderman Sallyanne Atkinson shot to international fame during her city's bid to host the 1992 Olympic Games, and in the process has forged herself a name as an exceedingly rare phenomenon; a woman who can cut the political mustard in a heavily, almost totally, male-dominated arena, and still maintain her charm, femininity, common sense and good humour.

Charismatic, a word possibly debased by current casual usage, would not be out of order to describe this undeniably personable and charming lady. Women who make it, against the odds, have never ceased to fascinate me. I personally have never harboured even the remotest political ambitions, basically I suppose because I am fundamentally apolitical, and also because after thirteen years working in international organizations I have developed a healthy cynicism as to where real power lies, and who is pulling policy strings. Seldom do politicans, except the few hard-nosed ones who muster the guts to make radical reforms in a post-landslide election honeymoon, generate the force to swim against a relentlessly efficient, self-protecting and self-propagating civil service. MI5/Heinemann case-watchers must now have come to the alarming conclusion that much of the real power in so-called democratic countries resides in the hands of a group of bureaucrats who feel themselves in no way accountable either to government, the electorate or indeed even to one another.

But we digress. Many male politicians evince fairly unedifying motives for seeking office. Some genuinely must feel that they are capable of doing something for the common weal, but many seem to be in the business for the endless possibilities of self-aggrandizement and lucrative scams.

Others feel, in passions of self-righteous zeal, that they know what is best for you and me, beliefs which I find perfectly unnerving. Motivation in the case of women, I would suggest, is often far simpler: they see what an appalling cock-up men have historically made, and feel, quite rightly, that they could do the job far better themselves.

In most instances there is very little which is venal, shoddy or second-rate in women politicians. In the European Parliament, for example, the institution of which I have most experience, there is a distressing quota of men who are avowedly in politics (if one can so describe what transpires at the European Parliament) for the rake-off, for the quick buck, for the far-from-niggardly expenses. There is little of that sentiment in the female contingent. Popular and gregarious Scottish Nationalist Winnie Ewing, for example, who represents the largest Euro-constituency, embracing the entire Highlands and Islands, actually loses money in her tireless efforts to visit all her constituents. In an entirely different political mould, there is former Labour Cabinet Minister, Barbara Castle, who despite her septuagenarian vintage remains impeccably well-groomed, and intellectually capable of knocking most of her rival Tory young turks or yuppity young Socialist whipper-snappers into a cocked hat. And, operating in quite a different political sphere, there is of course the British Prime minister, Margaret Thatcher, who French wags maintain is the only man in the British Cabinet. Consonant with Darwinian concepts of evolution, the fittest women in politics certainly look more capable of survival than an increasingly emasculated bunch of men.

From our British Iron Lady, we move back to Brisbane's Iron Frangipani, as Sallyanne has been so appositely named. She finds it all a huge joke, and is wearing a pair of frangipani earrings, enamel on gold, not exactly iron, but the self-deprecating humour is evident. Whereas a Margaret Thatcher or a Simone Veil would be reasonably labelled attractive women, Sallyanne Atkinson is positively pretty. Her bubbling sense of fun is also an endearing attribute those two remarkable political doyennes might do well to study. Gravitas never ranked particularly highly on my scale of human values.

I was the first visitor to her plush new suite of offices in City Hall, an impressive building built in 1930 which had been left to gather cobwebs since a previous incumbent vacated it some six years prior, and had subsequently been virtually locked to the public. The lady Lord Mayor had decided that this majestic edifice should be returned to the people of Brisbane, and should once again become a place where people want to congregate, 'a place which is warm, welcoming and alive'.

The storm clouds were starting to gather, however, with criticisms of over-spending and wasted rate-payers' money.

'Oh, I'm used to all that,' remarked Sallyanne, unperturbed. 'When I was trying to convince the International Olympic Committee that the Olympic Games should come to Brisbane I was obliged to travel all over the place, and people complained that I was never at home looking after the garbage collectors' dispute! We have now put Brisbane on the map. At least people know where we are, and how to pronounce the name.' (Bris-bun *not* Brisbane.)

Sallyanne is nothing if not a pragmatist. Of course she was disappointed that Brisbane had failed in its Olympic bid, but at least the episode had given her the opportunity to promote the city and the State.

'One of my strengths is that I can see the best in everything,' she admitted, as we looked at her collection of memorabilia, stopping over one of her prize exhibits – a bowlful of Scottish stones. Were those from her recent visit to Edinburgh, where she had handed over the Commonwealth Games flag to the luckless Scottish organizers? Brisbane had successfully hosted the games in 1982, and had hoped to use much of the existing sporting infrastructure to accommodate the Olympic Games.

'Oh, no,' she corrected my mistaken conclusion quickly, 'I've had those since the days when we lived in Scotland, at a time when my husband (a neuro-surgeon) was doing a stint of his training in Edinburgh. One of my daughters was even born there, on the National Health, and we let her keep her British nationality in case she ever wanted to swim for Scotland.'

Sallyanne's face erupts into smiles, at the aberration of the thought, and she starts to giggle.

'Unfortunately the Scottish swimmers got a lot better, and now for my daughter to be able to vote here in Australia, she will have to be naturalized.' She paused for a minute, obviously consigning that comment to some mental in-tray, a chore to be dealt with at a later stage.

By now the interview had developed into a tête-à-tête chat. We laughed about the aggressively new, and extremely inappropriate, visual display unit sitting defiantly white against the ceiling-to-floor leadlight windows overlooking King George Square. In amongst the 1930s furniture and light fittings, made to the design of the originals, it looked as incongruous as an outer-space man in the Long Room at Lord's. We both pretended to be computer-illiterate, the sort of games women play when all around them are men knowing only half as much as they do yet claiming to be experts.

'I think these things are counter-productive,' she remarked mischievously. 'Instead of the men in the office popping their heads around the door and giving you a message, they are all now busily sending one another memos on their computer terminals.'

It would appear that Sallyanne shares my doubts about men ever really growing up.

'I think women make ideal politicians,' she continued. 'I came into politics after I had raised a family and looked after a husband. When you've spent a few years with a baby in one arm, a toddler hanging on to your skirt, trying to stir the peas, stuff the chicken, open the door and answer the phone you have an excellent grounding in trying to deal with twenty people and a hundred problems all at once.'

I think that here Sallyanne has put her finger on one of the reasons why so few women make it to the top, and the very reason why they are such forces to be reckoned with if they do. Men are basically mono-conceptual. They tend to compartmentalize their day, their feelings, their thinking and their performance. We are all aware of the phenomenon of the man who slams the door behind him in the morning, entirely capable of forgetting his wife and his kids while he is in the office, completely capable of forgetting the office while he is on the rugger or cricket field, and more than totally capable of forgetting the lot of them while he is in the pub. A woman, meanwhile, has to play a juggling act with various interwoven lives throughout her normal day. If she has a career, even if it is as intellectually demanding and lucrative as her husband's, it will nevertheless be *her* responsibility to think about making a detour to the super-market before traipsing home, organizing Susie to visit the orthodontist to have the expensive ear-to-ear scaffolding checked, and ensuring that Johnnie gets to his lethal ju-jitsu class on time. Women rarely get to the top of the pile because of all these important yet trivial interferences in their lives. Women who have the energy to be world-beaters after these multifarious demands on their time and attention are generally unstoppable.

We are apparently now witnessing a new breed of man, however – Sensitive Man, the sort of man who helps with the children or considers giving the wife a hand with the dishes when he has been playing darts in the pub or punting in the betting shop all day, and she has just returned from Sainsbury's, the launderette and an eight-hour session lecturing in astro-physics. These chaps are already coming in for a lot of flak from the old macho types. Rumours abound that these softies use pH-balanced soap bars, exfoliating skin rubs, foaming face cleansers, astringent tonics and – is there no end to it? – moisturizers. Malevolent machos go so far as to suggest that these sensitive types even go down to the off-licence to fetch their own beer during Match of the Day. I mean, why else did the good Lord create women? Anyway, if Sensitive Man is alive and doing well somewhere, it must be recorded that he has not yet reached the portals of the Edmonds' household.

Men, of course, are not always the severest critics of high-profile women. It is often women, under-achieving women frightened that their comfortable and undemanding role as second best is being tacitly questioned by the Sallyannes of life, who are the most vicious. Certain types of redundant female who have nothing better to do with their lives than go to the hairdressers and organize their wardrobes are quick to pounce on outstanding members of their own sex. 'I've had women complain that they saw me wearing the same dress on two consecutive days, and that I was always wearing the same colours,' remarked Sallyanne, patently unconcerned. She had been, at the time, heavily involved in the final do-or-die-bid for the Olympics, lobbying in Lausanne for the East European vote, and giving stand-up interviews from six in the morning. I thought I ought to mention this, because re-reading what I have just written, in a quick burst of feminist furore, it might seem that I have little time for men. In effect, nothing could be further from the truth; some of my best hairdressers have been men. No! My utmost contempt on the contrary is definitely not reserved for any sort of man, but for a certain type of woman. She knocks around, even in cricketing circles. Oh, you will never have heard of her, of course; she will never have done anything of note in her life, except perhaps marry someone of whom she has become an added accessory. She will never have put her name to an article or a book, but you can bet your bottom dollar that the unattributed bitchy quotes in gossip columns will have come straight from her. Sweet as pie to everyone, she will grease up to selectors and committee men and do regular hatchet jobs on players and wives alike, or organize some feature artiste to do the dirty work for her. No, you have probably never heard of these females. They wear their doting maternity as a badge of care and concern, but from personal experience we all know these are the true vipers in any con-fraternity's bosom.

All politicians must, of course, learn to inure themselves to criticism. The good ones will listen to fair comment and disregard the rest, and the bad ones will disregard the lot. Not that listening to too many people is the best course of action either. Australian Prime Minister Bob Hawke, with his apparent policy of government by opinion polls, is at present doing little to impress the solid Labor base which originally swept him to power. As Lord Mayor of Brisbane, however, Sallyanne Atkinson is accountable directly and immediately to her electorate, and is proving a popular choice. Formerly a journalist, she has naturally winning ways with the media, and an engaging stock of anecdotes and accents. She relates with wry amusement her early days as a freelance reporter for some local Edinburgh paper, when for want of a babysitter she was obliged to drag the children along to an interview with some suitably august (at least in his own mind) municipal dignitary: 'I could see him thinking, "Who on earth is this woman?",' she recounts. Neither does she mind giving a very passable imitation of French Prime Minister and Mayor of Paris, Jacques Chirac. All French men love a pretty lady, and few pretty ladies are entirely unsusceptible to the intoxicating power of full-strength Gallic charm. Sallyanne and Jacques formed a mutual admiration society during their respective, unsuccessful quests for the Olympic Games, and the suave Gaullist even promised to visit Brisbane should the Lady Lord Mayor's bid succeed. 'A mayoralty, more than any other political office, represents something specific,' explained Sallyanne; 'the Mayor is very much the symbol of the town. Chirac is inextricably connected with Paris – in everybody's mind sophisticated, special.'

She too, this bright, warm, vivacious and engaging lady, has become a symbol of a new Brisbane, a forward-looking Brisbane, a city aiming to develop along the right lines to attract and encourage family businesses as well as vast corporate investment, to become the thriving heartland of a major tourist industry. 'I admire our Premier because he encourages private enterprise,' she claims. 'We are now witnessing a worldwide drift to the sun, aided by the fact that modern technology means people no longer need to live on top of their work. The recent expansion and investment in Queensland has been phenomenal.'

She is perfectly right. While we were in Queensland, ABTA, the Association of British Travel Agents, was being treated to some typically sumptuous Queensland hospitality up on the Gold Coast. Indeed, any British tourist who can overcome the psychological hurdle of a twenty-four-hour flight could do a lot worse than test the beaches, the shellfish, the climate and the sybaritic lifestyle so easily affordable out here. I sincerely hope we get the opportunity to return for a real holiday at the end of this exhausting tour. It is not a matter of sheer coincidence that the France/Australia Association has twinned Brisbane with Nice, that most exhilarating of all Mediterranean millionaires' playgrounds. The Mayor of Nice had recently been to Queensland to visit Sallyanne, and suggestions of starting a perfume industry, similar to the celebrated enterprises encouraged by the flower growers of Grasse, are currently under serious consideration. Perhaps the Iron Frangipani will shortly have her own personalized fragrance. She certainly deserves it. My abiding impression is that this woman could well scale the ultimate political heights, and if so, they had better watch out in Canberra. Sallyanne Atkinson, that potent combination of the pretty, the practical and the powerful, is no man's fool.

I left the Lord Mayor on the stone steps of the City Hall atrium, the choir from the local Girls' High School practising full-voiced for their end-of-term prize-giving, and the good burghers of Queensland's capital wandering in and out seeking municipal advice, or inspecting a local art and sculpture exhibition. Pope John Paul II would be arriving here within the week; the media hype and evangelical fervour were already starting to gather momentum. A practising Roman Catholic and an indefatigable promoter of her town, Sallyanne looked down on to her milling fellow citizens, and chalked up another plus for the city of Brisbane.

It was the Test match rest day, and so Phil and I hired a car and drove to Surfers' Paradise, a putative paradise on earth for those not particularly interested in Giovanni Paolo II's message of the more transcendental one in heaven. Perhaps it was a piece of pre-Papal visit Divine Intervention, but England were poised to win this match, their first win in eleven Tests. After their decidedly shabby performances thus far in State matches, the Australian media were beginning to wonder whether there had not been a deliberate ploy to confuse and confound the enemy. Ian Botham's quite remarkable display in a hard-hitting century during England's first innings would probably rank as the high note of the game. A consummate showman, perhaps second only to the Polish Pontiff himself, Botham has an unerring sense of exactly when and where to deliver the goods. Earlier in the tour, during England's match against Queensland, Botham had declared that he would be contracting himself to the State for the next two if not three years, and would be devoting his still remarkable talents to Queensland during the English winter months rather than being available for overseas tours. Botham's reasons were that he had made the decision for the sake of his wife and his family, which was difficult to comprehend since in England's *Sun* newspaper his wife was meanwhile declaring that she could not stand Australia, disliked the sun and blue skies, was extremely unhappy when she was here for four months a few years ago, would on no account disrupt her children's education, and had every intention of staying in England.

Whatever his motives, there is no doubt that Botham would do well in a place like Queensland. Jeff Thomson, another of Queensland's adoptive sons, has already claimed in his biography that Ian Botham would make a good Aussie, and the sort of outdoor, rugged, macho society which prevails in this State would appear to be on all fours with a Botham-genre temperament. Quite apart from all that, there are indisputably lucrative promotions contacts for the taking, and Botham's agent, Tom Byron, who is now a regular feature of this tour, is well on the way to making the jaded-with-touring-superstar a dollar-million-aire. Why on earth, at this stage of the game, spend uncomfortable and financially unrewarding months on tours to places such as Pakistan, the country Botham has described as 'the sort of place to send the mother-in-law', when mega-bucks can be commanded in this hedonists' Utopia?

Spectators and the press in particular will no doubt miss the 'Living Legend' (dixit Tom Byron), but it is, perhaps more than anything, the relentless invasions of the media into his colourful rock-star lifestyle that have precipitated Botham's decision. No more world media microscope. No more interminable private-life dissection. No more excoriating personality analyses in Queensland. I think he has made the right decision. Too bad for the British press. They have succeeded in killing the goose that laid their golden circulation eggs for the past decade. At thirty-one Ian Botham looks very much in danger of growing up, and one thing is for certain: he left the banana-benders at Brisbane's Gabba in no doubt that whatever investment might be ploughed into one I. T. Botham, it would all be money well spent.

It was a relief to see dear old Gower score a much overdue half-century, admittedly after having been granted a life early on. After inordinate amounts of media pressure, David has at least had some stripes, if not his former epaulettes restored, after being co-opted on to the selection committee. Phil thinks he is crackers to accept, feeling that it is a no-win situation. If the team does well, David will not share in the captain/vice-captain bouquets, and if the team screws it up, he will nevertheless be obliged to shoulder a proportion of the collegiate liabilities. My feeling is that he has been granted at least some token restoration of amour-propre, but, at the end of the day, Phil proved right.

The most poignant casualty thus far has been Nottinghamshire's perennially cheerful wicket keeper, Bruce French. Having stood with good-humoured patience in Paul Downton's shadow for so long, he has now been passed over in favour of the popular Cornishman, Jack Richards, in an effort to shore up the dicky higher-order batsmen. It is exactly the same phenomenon which we witnessed on our last tour to the West Indies. Specialist positions were sacrificed wholesale in increasingly frantic efforts to strengthen a tail which resolutely refused to wag. The itsy-bitsy selection policy of batsmen who can bowl a bit, and bowlers who can bat a bit, wicketkeepers who can balance a ball on their noses or catch a wet fish in their mouths a bit, seems a sure recipe for disaster. This series the Australian selectors too would appear to have embraced the philosophy with gusto.

Well, for the first Test at least, it very much looked as if one specialist left-arm orthodox spin bowler, Philippe-Henri Edmonds, was about to be sacrificed on the altar of selectorial mediocrity until the timely intervention of ex-England captain Tony Greig. I cherish memories of the tall, voluble South African being interviewed on his promotion to the England captaincy, his clipped, redolent of Piet Botha accent trilling almost Afrikaans-style, without the slightest trace of irony, 'I'm only proud to be captain of my country!'

It was, of course, the very same Tony Greig who masterminded the massive exodus of international cricketers to Kerry Packer's World Series cricket way back in 1977. The ensuing cleavage in the world of cricket, despite the sanctimonious cant from governing bodies everywhere, did not prove entirely deleterious to the financial prospects of all professional cricketers. A massive influx of hitherto untapped sponsors moved into traditional cricket, in attempts to stop the ever-increasing flow of players leaving for the Pyjama Game. Packer, whose erstwhile TV channel holds exclusive rights for the coverage of these 'Clashes for the Ashes', has been generous, even paternalistic, in finding jobs for the boys. Ian Chappell, Max (Tangles) Walker, Rodney Marsh and Greig all play major roles in the Test match commentaries, and in the Channel's sporting profile.

So it was that Greggie, who initiates the day's cricketing proceedings with a veritable armoury of incomprehensible technology (light meters, moisture meters, comfort meters, all but the Kennington Oval gaso meter), happened to meet England captain, Mike Gatting, inspecting the state of the wicket.

'You would be mad not to play two spinners,' said Greggie, knowing full well that England had every intention of playing just one, in the person of off-spinner John Emburey. The received wisdom at the Gabba is that pace bowlers do the damage, and far too many people whose job it is to think these things out for themselves demonstrate disturbing tendencies to rely exclusively on just such received wisdom.

The ex-England captain's advice was taken on board, and proved to be correct. Greig's philosophy, which is now gaining greater currency in both camps, is that you play your best players, almost irrespective of conditions. A wicket, even a wicket that looks positively Emerald Isle green on the first day, is often likely to change quite dramatically by the fourth and fifth. England won the Test match with no little help from spin, and as happens on these occasions, Gatting was hailed as a master tactician, and a profound thinker on the game.

However, back to Surfers' Paradise, a creation which epitomizes more or less everything that can go wrong when urban developers are given an excessively free rein. Although I did not actually spot any advertisements promising the dubious gastronomic and recreational pleasures of fish 'n' chips and a knees-up, the place nevertheless reminded me strongly of Torremolinos at the height of the season. Endless high-rise apartment blocks stood at stark right angles to the seashore, thus eliminating any semblance of a view for the further endless high-rise apartment blocks located just behind. We did not go surfing; Phil is hardly constructed in the 'Hang 10' mould. Instead we made our way to the new shopping/ eating/drinking complex, Fisherman's Wharf, where we bumped into the post-prandially very well-disposed David Gower with Allan Lamb and his wife Lindsay. Lindsay had just arrived in Queensland, via a very hard session with her plastic charge-card in Hong Kong. I had spoken to her on the phone in London just before my departure, when she had been working for some sheikh. 'I've got a switchboard the size of the organ at Westminster Abbey,' she groaned hyperbolically, 'and a typewriter the size of my double bed.'

It was good to see her again, although we both miss Alison Downton, a conjugal touring casualty along with husband Paul. Paul, now spending the winter months with stockbrokers James Capel, would actually be visiting us all at the first Test, on his round-the-world mission to flog British Gas shares. Every cloud has its silver lining. Paul, an extremely bright, affable and be-law-degreed cricketer, will do well in the City. It is far better, to my lights at least, to get out of the overseas tour rat-race before your thirties, and start an alternative career elsewhere. It is absolutely true that not all cricketers have the necessary grey matter to pursue such options, but if they do, even if it means missing out on the meretricious and transient buzz of international cricket, they must assuredly be far better off. England caps do not pay children's school fees. Neither do Man of the Match awards help forty-year-olds in the dole queue.

The lady Lord Mayor of Brisbane had remembered Mrs Lamb from her visit to London to watch Australia in the Davis Cup, in the days when Lindsay was on a nice little earner ferrying VIPs and tennis stars between their hotels and Wimbledon. Lindsay is genuinely a very funny woman, and Alison and I wept with laughter one lunchtime down the King's Road, as she regaled us with tales of decanting two bickering superstars on to the pavement, after advising them along with their twenty tennis rackets where to find the nearest tube station. I could just imagine her doing it to some 'you cannot be serious' super-brat, and watching him erupt.

The last day of the Test was a formality. I arrived in the press box to see England sweep to victory by eight wickets, and to witness the genuine jubilation in the British contingent. It makes life so much more pleasant for everybody, if admittedly a little dreary, when England are winning. There will be no newshounds flown in to do special investigative pieces on why individuals are not up to scratch if England's fortunes continue in this vein.

I am finding quite enough to keep me busy this tour with a fortnightly diary column for *The Times* back home in London, and regular phone-ins for London's Capital Radio. And then once a week it is the five-in-the-morning start for a breakfast TV spot on Channel 10's *Good Morning, Australia*, not to mention the *Not the Test Match* report for ABC national radio. Then there are features for the ever-expanding Murdoch group of papers, News Corporation Ltd, pieces which are syndicated all over the country, thus satisfying my neurotically megalomaniac desire for ubiquity. Apart from all that, of course, there is this here diary.

I felt it, therefore, almost perfectly justifiable that I should be awarded my colours, my media accreditation medal, by press gang leader Peter Smith during a touching little ceremony in the entrance hall of the Brisbane Crest Hotel. It is a piece of memorabilia I shall treasure all my life, especially since it took the combined efforts of *The Times* sports editor, Tom Clarke, and *The Times* editor Charlie Wilson to acquire it for me. It is a green-and-cream enamel-on-gilt artefact, three wickets superimposed on an outline of Australia, this interesting artistic perspective crowned by two crossed writing quills and placed into full aesthetic focus by the legend 'Australian Cricket Board'. Underneath, more gilt on cream, the word MEDIA glisters, patently not gold, and balances lintel-like over a removable base metal stopper proclaiming the vintage '87'. Said medal may be affixed to the person, or indeed to any other expedient protrusion, by means of a green cord. It was, as I say, an emotional scene, as memories of Mother Mary Paul, Order of St Ursuline, came flooding back to me, as she pinned my House Captain's badge to my palpitating-with-emotion bosom. 'And if you lose this, you've had it,' said Mother Mary Paul. 'And if you lose this, you've had it,' said Mr Peter Smith.

It would not look entirely the thing in the Givenchy accessories boutique at the George V, Paris, but I wear my medal with pride on the *de rigueur* Gucci handbag. If I stay twenty-five years in this profession, I shall probably have one made up in marcasite, like they do at 'M and S'.

I was not the only person to receive a medal that week. Australian captain, Allan Border, was awarded some gong on the first day of the Test match for services to sport, and took his rightful place amongst the Aussie pantheon of sporting deities. But the gods have a way of dealing cruel blows; Allan Border, national hero on the first day of the Test, had been metamorphosized into Allan Border, call me Grumpy, by the fifth.

It is unfortunate that I cannot give you an eye-witness account of Border's allegedly surly behaviour to the press, nor of his refusal to participate in the post-match hanging of heads and wringing of hands. There are apparently certain well-worn, penitential rights defeated captains are supposed to observe, certain acts of contrition they are obliged to perform, certain major confessions of error they are expected to make, and certain very firm purposes of amendment they are encouraged to promise if they are to have the slightest hope of media forgiveness. Poor Border. He apparently had not heard the rules, or if he had, was not inclined to play by them that particular day. I for one would certainly not blame him. People grovelling all over you one day, and trying simultaneously to stab you in the back and bonk you on the head the next, it is a wonder the man has not been consigned to some dark room with very soft walls, to go absolutely schizoid. All this, however, is mere hearsay. Despite my media *passe-partout* medal, despite press passes and accreditations a-go-go, despite the vicarious clout of the entire Murdoch empire, there was no way I was going to be allowed into that post-Test match press conference.

It would, at this juncture, be facile to rant about these backward Queensland gatemen in particular, and about sex discrimination and male chauvinist pigs in general. (Sad to relate, however, the same thing is equally likely to occur at that apogee of enlightened NW8 civilization, Lord's.)

'You cannot come in here,' commanded the withered, leathery, petrified geriatric old gargoyle guarding the picket gate with Cerberus-like ferocity. I have met these mini-Hitlers all over the world, and am convinced that obnoxious stupidity must have become a basic requirement for employment in cricket grounds everywhere. I showed him my multifarious media credentials; Peter Roebuck argued that I was his wife; other members of the press corps awarded Roebuck the George Medal for irresponsible courage; the gateman's obdurate 'niet' would not alter. 'You cannot come in here,' he repeated mantra fashion; 'you are a lady.'

There were at least a dozen British pressmen prepared to jump to my defence, and to testify to the mendacity of such a wild allegation. By this stage, however, Mike Gatting was making his stirring victory speech, proclaiming how 'nice' it was, indeed, how 'always nice' it was to win a Test match. I decided to husband my aggression for a better cause and moment. This shrivelled, apoplectic creature was no worthy adversary, and that triumphant day I did not feel inclined to wage the war of equal employment opportunities on behalf of the entire oppressed female population of Queensland.

As a codicil to this episode, however, there is one general point that crosses my mind. The worst discrimination against most women is generally meted out by both men and women who are socially, intellectually or educationally inferior to the women they discriminate against. The worst instances of discrimination, all women know, are perpetrated by the likes of gatemen, waitresses, barmaids and a certain breed of air hostess. Phil says I am super-sensitive, but it is all right talking about other folk being super-sensitive when you have never been subjected to the phenomenon yourself.

My pet aversion is the sort of air hostess who wheels the newspaper trolley down the Business Class section . . . 'Paper, sir? *The Times . . . Financial Times . . .* ?' she smirks to all those dirty old men trying surreptitiously to get on with their *Playboy* magazines.

In the meantime you, one of the relatively few women in Business Class, look up furtively from your Marcel Proust, trying hopefully to catch her glassy, over-made-up, male-oriented eye, and are tacitly made to understand, by a sequence of special air-hostess body language, that you are not deemed to be capable of so much as reading the in-flight sick bag. Some of my worst tantrums have been precipitated by such behaviour, and I can see the well-coddled male contingent thinking, 'What a bitch . . . dear little air hostess has so much to do . . .'

Of course, when travelling with an England cricket team, or indeed I suppose with any group of relatively young and athletic sportsmen, a woman would have to go into cardiac arrest before attracting the attention of the average air hostess. Our domestic flight carrier, in terms of adminis-tration, baggage handling and the general organization, has been superb. One occasion on the in-flight, however, I saw some of the most blatantly off-hand service ever witnessed, and I have flown Aeroflot. An entire section of the plane waited patiently for its plastic lunch, and – in my case – not quite so patiently for its in-flight alcoholic drink, one hostie regaled two not entirely disinterested members of the team with her contact addresses and telephone numbers for the next two months. Meanwhile an old lady with a stick hobbled down the aisle, unassisted, to the WC. Phil had to restrain me from lodging a complaint with the Purser. The England team was getting its flights heavily subsidized, if not more or less gratis. Frankly, I did not care. I was not, and neither was the handicapped old girl. All the more reason for us to be given if not priority, then at least equal treatment.

'Come off it, Frances,' remonstrated Phil. 'If a team of men is on a plane, it is totally understandable that the cabin crew will make a beeline for them.'

Understandable, it may well be. Acceptable, never.

Discrimination in its minor manifestations can be irritating. In its worst excesses it may be a moral canker that society would prefer to camouflage and forget. Perhaps that is why the West is perversely comfortable with the South African situation. What on earth would we do without apartheid? It is so much easier to pontificate righteously about the motes in other nations' eyes when the alternative is to contemplate the beams in our own. In international fora, for instance, the British, who are as consummate hypocrites as the next nation, are the first to decry the treatment of Jewish dissidents in the USSR, but will obstinately vet discussion on discrimination against the Roman Catholic minority in Northern Ireland as foreign interference in the United Kingdom's domestic affairs.

It must be on that understanding that any outsider ventures to address the vexed issue of Aboriginal and Islander ethnic minorities in Australia. Let's face it. We are *all* fed expurgated and nationalistically biased accounts of history. Mussolini, Stalin and Hitler even had the history books re-written in order to shore up their own political and social philosophies. Often, history has been recast to salve consciences, to exonerate the men from heinous crimes committed in the past, to whitewash behaviour which would be totally unacceptable by any current moral standard. The history of the Aboriginal people is a case in point.

It is worthwhile considering, for starters, that whereas 'Australia' will be celebrating its bicentenary in 1988, Aborigines have inhabited the continent for well over thirty thousand years. 1988, more significantly, not only represents two hundred years of European settlement, but it is also the twenty-first birthday of Aboriginal 'emancipation'. Difficult though it is to believe, it is only since 1967 that Aborigines have been counted as human beings on the census, and given the right to vote. It certainly puts drinks trolleys, newspapers and air hostesses in their proper perspective.

In terms of brash statistics, about one-and-a-half per cent to two per cent of Australia's population are Aboriginal or Islander, of whom about one-third live in Queensland. In Brisbane I visited the Queensland and Torres Strait Islander Consultative Committee and was shocked by some of the literature even a day's perusal in their library turned up. It was only in 1977, for example, that Aboriginal workers were given wages for their labour on reserves, rather than rations. We are talking about a mere decade ago! Going back eighty years, we find a member of the new Commonwealth Parliament stating in 1902: 'There is no scientific evidence that the Aboriginal is a human being at all.'

And in 1891, *The Boomerang* commented on the reported shooting of an Aborigine thus:

'Why bother us . . . with everyday commonplaces like this? Has it come to this in Australia, that the taking off of a solitary black fellow is to be wired all over this island continent? Have coloured persons ceased to be national game?'

And even worse, an ex-Education Minister of Tasmania, who declared that: 'Aborigines have less (*sic*) rights than kangaroos.' (Personally I feel that Education Ministers who say 'less' when they mean 'fewer' would do better to keep their mouths shut, and, with sentiments such as those, perhaps for good.)

Generations of politicians, governments and historians have all worked hard at sanitizing the true story of European settlement. Aborigines could be summarily executed as criminals if they so much as endeavoured to stop settlers invading and taking over their ancestral lands. The countless atrocities perpetrated against the indigenous population have been historically bowdlerized, however, and even in his speech introducing the Aborigines Act of 1971, the Minister, the Hon. N. T. E. Hewitt, professed to believe that: 'Smallpox was almost certainly the mass killer of Aboriginal people, and however much some of us might lust for murderous forebears, whose sins we might repay in an orgy of self-abasement, blame must be substantially allocated to their bacteria rather than muskets.'

This is as may be, but even in the course of my brief research as an historian (if I can be called an historian, or even a writer), I was able to discover otherwise. It might not have gone amiss if some parliamentary researcher had bothered to note that between 1824 and 1900 over ten thousand Aborigines were brutally murdered in Queensland alone, and many more *besides* died from diseases introduced by the European settlers.

The list of crimes against humanity is endless, and modern Australians were truly horrified to have their social consciences shaken by ABC Television's production of *The Secret Country*, an historical reconstruction of events, produced by John Pilger. Gradually more and more of the settlers' obscenities are being unearthed: incidents such as young Aboriginal children being buried up to their necks in sand, whilst mounted Europeans played polo with the protruding heads they managed to knock off.

Suffice it to say, the early European settlers were as guilty of genocide as Hitler's Nazis. In 1788 there were over five hundred distinct Aboriginal and Islander ethnic and language groups; now there are fewer than two hundred. It is perhaps the white man's worst disease, ethnocentricity: wipe out everything and anything that is not exactly like you. Invaders always endeavour to eradicate a subjugated nation's language early on, since they realize that with the language goes the entire cultural heritage and identity of the ethnic minority. Even today, many Aboriginal children are obliged to learn through the medium of English – their second language, and a language often inadequate for the expression of certain cultural and intellectual concepts shared by all Aboriginal communities.

It is without doubt this fundamental difference in outlook and values which continues to divide the ethnic minorities from the white majority today. At the root of the cultural divide lies the two societies' diametrically opposed perceptions of land, and its use. Land for white, essentially capitalist society is a tool, an asset to be worked and exploited for further increase of wealth. Aboriginal society perceives land as something more spiritual – life itself. It is this basic antagonism between the European quick-buck philosophy and the more transcendental Aboriginal ethos which lies at the root of Australia's most serious running sore, of the wound current politicians would rather veil with thin gauze than dress properly. The Aboriginal land rights issue sadly is not a vote-catcher.

Since the arrival of the Europeans, Aborigines have been hounded from their tribal homelands. Land to the Aboriginal people means far more than somewhere to graze sheep, rear cattle, mine bauxite, or even the far more lucrative uranium. Land means the source and the locus of life. It represents the eternal nature of the spirit. By removing land from the Aborigines, Europeans were doing far more than physically expropriating them. As Professor W. E. H. Stenner wrote:

> 'Particular pieces of territory, each a homeland, formed part of a set of constants without which no affiliation of any person to any other person, no link in the whole network of relationships, no part of the complex structure of social groups, any longer had all its co-ordinates.'

It never crossed any State Premier's mind, not even in his wildest socially-concerned moments, that Aborigines should be entitled to compensation of any sort for the real estate that had been wrested from them, and these people have been kicked, from reserve post to settlement pillar, for almost two hundred years now.

What is ironically worse is that the land they were grudgingly allowed to live on, courtesy of the fact that it was unsuitable for agriculture, has often proved to be rich in minerals. What the farmer would not touch, the mining experts have grabbed. So it was in Mapoon, where bauxite, the raw material for aluminium, was found in the 1950s and 1960s. The Aborigines refused to leave their lands, and so the police moved in, set fire to their settlements, and cleared the land for the mining companies Comalco and Alcan. Collusion between the Queensland Government and the mining companies was scandalously repeated at Aurukun in 1975, when the Government again made free with other people's land. This incident created far more international consternation, since the anti-nuclear lobby became involved. This time the more controversial end product was to be uranium.

Even as I write, a fierce battle is raging in the Northern Territories over the fate of Kakadu National Park, where mining companies could well do irreparable ecological damage as well as ruin centuries-old Aboriginal cave paintings.

The Labor administration, whose political fortitude over such issues bears all the hallmarks of a confectionery jellybaby, but without the backbone, is still vacillating on the fence of political expediency, presumably still deciding on which side the more votes lie; in fact, I asked Bob Hawke about his government's track record on Aboriginal land rights a few weeks later, at the Prime Minister's XI v. England one-day invitation match at Canberra. In March of 1986, the Minister for Aboriginal Affairs, Clyde Holding, announced the Federal Labor Government's decision to dump the idea of implementing National Land Rights Legislation. With this complete volte-face, the Federal Government effectively abandoned Australian Labor Party (ALP) policy and the five basic principles embodied therein. Those principles, outlined by Holding in Geneva in 1984, one year after Labor swept to power, are Aboriginal control over mining and mining royalties in their lands, compensation for lost lands to be negotiated, guaranteed inalienable freehold title and the protection of freehold sites.

The Federal Government, in truth, caved in under the enormous economic pressure of the mining and agricultural lobbies. Mr Hawke, busily watching David Gower bat, would admit to no such thing.

'We have decided to leave such issues to State governments,' he explained. 'If we do things at Federal level, there is generally a backlash against the Aboriginal population in each State. I believe that the Aborigines themselves know that is true.'

Oh, dear Bob, really! Surely you must know that most States' past performances have demonstrated a lack of generosity and compassion in dealing with this question which posits the absolute necessity for Federal intervention? As I have already mentioned, however, Aboriginal issues, and it bears repeating, are not a vote-catcher. Well-publicized cocktail parties, hob-nobbing with international cricketers at The Lodge, most definitely are.

There are few politicians nowadays, however, who have the stature to be guiltless of such blatant expediency. Perhaps, with our present democratic system of government by media approval, there is none left at all.

If a self-professed Labor government refuses to grasp this uncomfortable political nettle, the future looks bleak indeed for a group of people who want neither to be eliminated, nor segregated, nor protected, nor assimilated, nor subjected to any of the white-conceived policies mis- and dis-informed bureaucrats dream up on their behalf. They merely want to the right to be equal and different. In a country as large as Australia, surely this need not be too much to ask.

It is easy on a cricket tour to remain immured from the harsher social and political realities of the host country. In India, for example, in order to survive the visual assaults of poverty and misery, it is almost imperative to scurry for the cosmopolitan tranquility of the hermetically sealed Intercontinental Hotel. Conversely, on the island paradises of the West Indies all but the most assiduously high-minded

1. 'G' day from WA', The America's Cup: Harold Cudmore, skipper of *White Crusader* (right); me (at helm); unknown onlooker.

2. Not the MI5 trial. Neil and Romany Foster (Gutter Press) and Peter Lush (QC) at the Christmas party.

3. Two convivial Australians.

4. The Sugar-Plamb Fairies, Allan and Lindsay.

5. Deparment of Health and Social Security, Melbourne.

6. 'Prime Minister, would you mind leaving the Ambassador, walking down to the fence and squinting a bit with the sun in your eyes, so I can get some cricket in this shot?' Adrian Murrell, All-Sport photographer.

7. 'This should keep her quiet for a minute.'

8. 'Yes, Fender! Another duck!'

may remain jovially oblivious to the internecine political wrangling and the socio-economic strife being played out all around. Similarly, in a country such as Australia, with its generalized affluence and widespread well-being, the Aboriginal issue would escape most tourists, indeed even most Australians', attention. Few Aborigines stray from their reserves. Those who become urban dwellers are generally involved in menial tasks, selling newspapers on street corners and the like. The incidence of drunkenness and petty crime is disturbingly high in this disaffected, vagrant population, and the statistics on Aboriginal deaths in police custody even more so. Until such times as these gentle, childlike and noble people are allowed the right to live somewhere on their own vast continent in peace and prosperity. Australian governments must hang their heads in shame.

Back at the Gabba a victorious England cricket team was making very merry. Past player/press antagonisms and paranoias were, at least temporarily, forgotten, as the captain invited the British confraternity of cricketing scribblers into the dressing room for celebratory champagne. Notable by their absence were Thicknesse of 'boorish bully' fame, and Johnson of 'can't bat, can't bowl and can't field' notoriety. Not that either of them was necessarily wrong in what he had penned, of course, but no one cares who or what is right or wrong when a team has just won.

Everyone in the media has developed an exaggerated tendency to focus exclusively on the exploits of Ian Botham. Truth to tell, his was a magnificent century, but people often forget other equally worthwhile contributions by other less high-profile players. John Emburey, for example, took five wickets in the second innings, on a track not hitherto noted as a spinners' wicket, and many correspondents felt that he, along with Botham, should have shared in the Man of the Match award. Interestingly enough, there is little indication that any of the team resents the excessive attention devoted to Botham. Perhaps recent past history has demonstrated that the media microscope is a double-edged sword, and few players would welcome the degree of personal-history exposure to which Beefy is constantly subjected. That is the obverse of the very lucrative coin.

England at last seem to have found a happy opening combination in Bill Athey and Chris Broad. Bill seems a quiet, thinking and serious chap. I notice he sometimes appears rather impatient with the puerile laughs and japes which so characterize our coach transfers to and from airports, and he has my every sympathy. Chris is a tall, strong, good-looking lad, the combination of patience and confidence which hallmarks the best opening bats. Another gem discovery is Leicestershire's West Indian-born all-rounder, Phillip DeFreitas, whose most endearing quality is his patent and untrammelled joy in the game. It is heartening to see these born-talented rookies enjoying their cricket before all the clever-dick experts start coaching them. Remember Middlesex and England's Norman Cowans before Willis *et al*, with all the best will in the world, succeeded rather splendidly in mangling him?

Cowans, incidentally, a former England paceman, is currently being sued by a Brisbane cricket club, Wests, for breach of contract. Wests' players sought the Jamaican-born bowler's services for the Australian summer and pooled their resources to meet his demands for air fares, accommodation and 'suitable' employment. Cowans, however, flew back to England after featuring in merely one-and-a-half games, citing flood damage to his London apartment as the reason for his hasty departure. Pursuant to contract, his air fares had indeed been paid, and accommodation had been found in the home of Wests' captain, John Bell. Perhaps Norman's precipitate departure may have been related to the suggested employment the club had found fit to organize for him – as a bouncer at the local night club. This is probably a salutary tale for young players seeking overseas jobs to while away an English off-season. Job descriptions from twelve thousand miles away, verbal contracts over the phone and flights into the unknown are a professional cricketer's Russian roulette.

Another Middlesex casualty this tour looks set to be Wilf Slack. Phil, who has seen Wilf play over many seasons, is naturally heavily biased in his favour, but the West Indian-born opening batsman has done nothing to impress thus far, and is probably destined now to be side-lined for some time. It is so desperately depressing for those members of the team who know that, barring injury, or a cataclysmic collapse or phantom pregnancies in the team, they are likely to be spending little time in the middle. Wilf is obviously upset, but bears everything with a remarkable degree of stoicism. The boys have nicknamed him 'Bishop Tutu' (I rather think that South African-born Allan Lamb was at the genesis of this), and Slack plays up to the title with tireless good humour. Somehow Legga (Lamb) prevailed upon him the other day to carry his kit and ghettoblaster on to the bus.

'They can't seem to get bossing out of their systems, these people,' grinned Tutu. Earlier on in the tour, sweating together collegiately in a sauna, Lamb had asked Wilf to throw some more water on to the steaming charcoal. 'Do it yourself,' rejoined Tutu immediately; 'we're not in Soweto now, you know.'

The rest of the West Indian contingent have been awarded floral tags. Pencil-slim DeFreitas goes by the name of 'Daffy' and Gladstone Small, inevitably cops 'Gladdy' or 'Glad'. David Gower has been granted a further sobriquet to add to his motley collection. Percy Fender, Jardine's patrician predecessor as captain of Surrey, was apparently wont to travel the country with his own cases of claret in tow. David, whose proclivities in matters vinous and especially Bordeaux are equal to my own, is thus referred to as 'Fender'. I do believe he has put down a cellar of some six hundred bottles in his Leicestershire home, and I most certainly did my best to create a dent in it earlier in the year, at a barbecue David and his fiancée, Vicki, threw during a Test match at Edgbaston.

Yes, it is all very, very merry in the England camp at the moment, which I do believe goes to prove that all the talk about team spirit and good morale is the most unutterable hog-wash. Winning teams exhibit these phenomena, losing teams do not. Forget about how they are playing the game; everything depends on whether they win or lose.

Conceivably the tiniest of serpents had wiggled its way into the Garden of Eden that is currently the England dressing-room. The Federal Government had just launched a nationwide 'Operation Noah', by which friends, relations or even acquaintances may ring a toll-free number, and inform the police of drug offenders they know, and their reprehensible habits. Colloquially referred to as the 'dob-in-a-mate' operation, it may possibly have caused the odd quiet shiver down the odd victorious English spine, but who will ever know?

Down the road from the Gabba, England were involved in yet another victory, against Australia and against good taste. I had first heard about the sport of 'dwarf-tossing' when it came up as a Motion for a Resolution to be debated by the European Parliament in Strasbourg. The EuroParl has never exactly been immune from involving itself in abstruse debates, wacky even by international organization standards, but this one definitely took *le biscuit*. Had it not been moved by an eminently sensible and conscientious Italian woman, Signora Vera Squarcialupi, who sits with the Communists and Allies, it would probably have been passed over as the Euro equivalent of an April Fool's Day wheeze. As it was, the European Parliament dealt with it in a duly concerned, indeed outraged fashion, and solemnly called upon the Australian Government to put an end to this offensive practice immediately.

Dwarf-tossing, as the name implies, involves the tossing of persons of diminutive stature by persons of less restricted growth. I fail to remember the exact terms of the European Parliament's Motion for Resolution, but in all probability it went something like this: The European Parliament –

having regard to the United Nations Convention on Human Rights

having regard to the treaty establishing the European Coal
and Steel Community

having regard to the treaty establishing the European
Atomic Energy Community

having regard to the treaty establishing the European Economic Community

having regard to anything else your research assistant can
come up with

whereas it is naughty to toss dwarves about

whereas you would not like it if they did it to you, would
you?

whereas Snow White would never have behaved like that,
would she?

calls upon the Australian Government to put an end to this
deplorable recreation immediately (otherwise we may have
to send you yet another inter-parliamentary delegation, and
you wouldn't want that, would you?) and *instructs* the President of the European Parliament to find a stamp and send
it off to Bob Hawke (if he's not in his office, you'll probably
find him on the golf course) as soon as possible.

Dwarves involved in the sport were apparently not unanim-
ously delighted with the EuroParl's unsolicited interference
in their chosen profession, and some even went so far as to
claim that, *ab contrario*, it was their fundamental human
right to be tossed around if they so desired. Legal eagles
were quickly briefed to argue that any effort deployed to
stop a dwarf being tossed might constitute a restriction of
trade, with all that that implied in terms of compensation
for loss of earnings.

And so the battle continued to rage, as the England
versus Australia dwarf-tossing Test series got off to a start
at Brisbane's Manhattan nightclub. A variation called dwarf
rolling has apparently also been devised by the promoters.
This involves the unfortunate dwarf being strapped to a
skateboard and rolled head first at a set of ninepins. It

seems as if in Queensland, at least, the age of the circus freak show is still going strong.

Happily, pressure from the public, the police and the Little People Association of Australia seems to have resulted in the cancellation of the rest of the 'Test' series. A tasteless and undignified sport which holds little people up to ridicule, it nevertheless attracts a good following here in certain Aussie circles. This is also the country where another particular sub-species of man feels the need to get his rocks off watching virtually naked women wrestling in cream. With all the competition, it is no wonder the Australian selectors are having difficulties in cobbling together a quality Test team.

Talking about virtually naked women, and incidentally a competition feminists find equally as offensive as dwarf tossing, I noticed from a television newsreel that Miss Trinidad and Tobago had won the 1986 Miss World Competion. A couple of months ago, I too received an invitation from organizer Eric Morley to grace the event. 'Would you consider participating in the Miss World Competition?' he had written (my spirits rose as I reached for the peroxide and the Clearasil) . . . 'as the interpreter?'

The circus was on the road again the next day for a State match against New South Wales in Newcastle. Pope John Paul II had taken precedence over the England team and had been granted the Sydney Cricket Ground, so we were off to the sticks. Quite right, too: one, he is a better performer, and two, he draws larger crowds. It was difficult to tell whether the other great showman and crowd-puller, Beefy Botham, was disturbed over the recent news from Shepton Mallet, where eighteen hundred Somerset supporters had voted in favour of their Committee's decision to sack Joel Garner and Viv Richards, and a mere eight hundred had voted against. Despite his avowed intention of resignation should his two mates be axed, he did not look like a man with no options.

5

Perth via Newcastle

We arrived in Newcastle on a cold, miserable and rainy day. Imagine, if you will, Newcastle, England, on a cold, miserable and rainy day. Got it? Well, here you have Newcastle, New South Wales, on a cold, miserable and rainy day. They manufacture steel here, lots of it. They have difficulties with production levels and they have aggro with unions. Yes, it is just the same as back home.

Our bedroom in the Settlers Motor Inn overlooked Newcastle beach, where, weather permitting, the international surfing festival would be taking place over the weekend. A few days prior, a youngster had been struck by a bolt of lightning (which flashed, so we were told, out of a clear blue sky), and survived to tell the tale. The incident constituted the main topic of conversation in the hotel's dining-room, where just about every waitress had been an eye-witness. 'He died three times on the way to hospital,' said one, wondering whether we wanted *mange tout* peas or salad; 'third-degree burns all over him,' she added, pouring out the Cabernet Sauvignon. 'Horrible it was, horrible.' My rare, charcoal-grilled steak looked decidedly less appetizing.

After their victory in the first Test, England were back to form, failing to score two hundred runs against New South Wales in the first innings. Acting captain John

Emburey was moved to attempt some stirring rhetoric in his early-morning pre-match pep talk. The motivating effects of Embers' earnest, morale-boosting efforts were not immediately apparent. One ex-England captain lay prostrate on his back, eyes closed, obstinately oblivious to all around him. The non-verbal comments of another former England captain could be heard reverberating sonorously from the dressing-room's WC, and he added for good measure that any rah-rah sentiments he had ever harboured were long since down the pan.

Not content with the mediocrity of their first innings' performance, England managed to get themselves bowled out for eighty-three in the second. The crowd had been promised a one-day game to compensate for the truncated State match, if a result could be achieved by a certain deadline. Both teams' blatant time-wasting ensured that the NSW victory came after the bewitching hour, and supporters felt, quite rightly, that they had been conned.

Despite appalling storms and gales during the week, the Sabbath weather turned out to be a glorious 33°C, and the wind and waves ideal for the surfing carnival. The beach was packed from the early hours of the morning, with brightly coloured tents and flags festooning the shoreline.

The day began brilliantly, and got progressively better. An extraordinarily intrusive public-announcements system relayed information of mindless banality. Every five minutes we were told it was a beautiful day. Looking up at the peerless blue sky, most of us had already figured that one out for ourselves. Then we were introduced to one of the competitors, a certain Mr Wesley Lane, who apparently hailed from the east coast of California. There is obviously a lot of good surf on the east coast of California. We were reminded in between every commercial break that we were having a great day. Again, I prefer to make such decisions for myself rather than have them foisted on me by some recycled disc jockey.

In fairness, however, it *was* a good day. The surfers were all physically perfect creatures, not a hint of excess adipose tissue, just muscles in places where lesser mortals don't even have places. Their heaving torsos, honed to physical perfection thanks to years of self-sacrifice devoted to becoming total beach bums, palpitated against their rubber wet suits. Flashes in contrasting colours running down their sides and legs further accentuated the tree-trunk thighs and the Grecian-urn-shaped legs. There were lots of sun-bleached locks in evidence, crowning extensive suntans.

The male surfers were not all that bad either, peripatetic Adonises well-tried in catching waves and 'hanging 10' all over the world. The crowd went wild as Tom Curren of the United States, and Australia's Mark Occhilupo hit the water for the BHP Steel International final, to be contested between the two top seeds. Occhilupo, the local crowd's favourite, emerged the victor, and Lolita surfing groupies wobbled dangerously in and indeed out of their bikinis as he took the podium to make his acceptance speech.

Dear me! Serious error! The pitch of his voice seemed to suggest a wet suit perhaps two or three sizes too small, and the hard-earned macho image took a dreadful nose-dive. The crowds dispersed, wind-burned, sun-burned, some slightly sloshed, eskies (Oz for cold box) empty. Yes, it had been a good day at the Surfest on Newcastle beach.

The very first surfers in the world, as it happened, were the Aborigines of Kahibah and Lake Macquarie, not far from Newcastle. They were members of the Awabakal tribe, who came to the area for their tribal sporting events, and combined surfing, swimming and canoe races with tree-climbing and boomerang-throwing. Few people realize that the first team of Australian cricketers to tour England (in 1868) was made up of Aborigines. They played five days a week for five months, with only eleven players on tour. Play started at 11 a.m. and continued until at least 7 p.m., with no afternoon tea-break. Travel between matches was by horse-drawn carriage, on very rough roads, but even this punishing schedule could not diminish the team's enthusiasm. The Aborigines had a reputation for bright cricket, and played just like modern West Indian teams.

Their fielding particularly was remarkable, with one of the outstanding all-rounders, Mullagh, able to throw a ball over a hundred yards. Nicknames such as 'Mosquito' and 'Twopenny' solved English and indeed Australian scorers' problems in spelling tribal names, and of the forty-seven matches played on that tour, the Aborigines won fourteen and drew nineteen. It's surprising to relate how little has changed in terms of schedules since 1868!

On their return to Australia the Aborigines played three matches, the receipts of the last one ear-marked as recompense for their five-month slog overseas. Unfortunately the weather proved so hot that people failed to show up, and the team emerged poorly rewarded for their sporting achievements.

The men never played as a team again, although some did play for local clubs, and when Mullagh died in 1891, he had his bat and his cricket stumps buried with him. In the circumstances, the current Australian selectors should start sending scouts out into the bush to look for a few talented Aborigine hopefuls, and integrate them into the green-and-gold uniform, just as the English have done with our naturally athletic West Indian-born players. The all-white Australian team certainly looks in need of a good injection of ethnic zip and zest.

Next stop Perth via a change-over at Sydney. This time we are staying at the Merlin Hotel, a monumental piece of architecture, with the bedrooms and corridors all over-looking one vast atrium. The swimming pool here is a definite improvement on the Sheraton-Perth, where by some logistic aberration the pint-sized pond has been located in the shadow of the hotel. Manager Peter Lush has been tireless in putting his PR and marketing skills to good use on this trip, and has managed to negotiate far better rates for the team at the more luxurious Merlin than they were getting at the Sheraton.

Peter is a large, jovial and prematurely grey man. By the end of the tour he will no doubt be prematurely even greyer. His two greatest assets are a lot of common sense, an attribute not always overwhelmingly in evidence back home at HQ, and a fairly well-developed sense of humour. The day after our arrival, he asked me, tongue in cheek, whether I intended to watch the boys practising in the nets. Since assistant manager Micky Stewart is obliged to devote the entire gamut of his persuasive techniques to encouraging the team to watch themselves practising in the nets, my supernumerary attendance seemed clearly above and beyond the call of duty. Besides, the siren song of the twelve-metre yachts was calling irresistibly from Fremantle: the French pavement cafes, the Italian pizzerias, the American bars, the British pubs and all those genuinely rippling biceps. As a real treat, our mate Spud Spedding invited us to go sailing with the trial horse, *White Crusader II*, affectionately known as Hippo.

The crews were at the time in a lay period, prior to the commencement of the elimination round for the semi-finals. The British crew were testing spinnakers and we followed initially in the twenty-knot breeze aboard the tender *James Capel* – guess who was sponsoring that little contribution to the British effort. It was an exhilarating experience, and provided some inkling of how the conditions would be when the notorious Fremantle Doctor arrived.

It is oh-so infra-dig in Australia at the moment to maintain that watching twelve-metre yacht racing is about as interesting as watching grass grow or paint dry. However, for moribund matrons such as myself whose expectations of the Elysian Fields revolve around the possibility of staying in bed all day watching the cracks in the ceiling, this need not necessarily constitute derision. Such assertions, nevertheless, are completely unjustified. The more the knowledge of any sport, the more the enjoyment, and quite apart from any other consideration, the physical buzz of following a twelve-metre race must constitute one of the best spectator outings ever: cloudless blue skies, the open air, the sun beating down on a constantly oscillating grey/green/azure ocean, the wind in your hair, the spray in your face, the salt in your blood, a glass in your hand . . . there are few better sports to be viewed from the periphery.

Over in the distance was Yanchep Sun City, one of Perth entrepreneur Alan Bond's earliest ventures in real estate. Originally Bond's 'Home of the Twelves', Alan's successive crews were not upset when he moved his marina further into Fremantle. To the delight of local fishermen, not suitably conscious of the future honours to be bestowed upon the Bond syndicate, the glut of seaweed in the waters around Yanchep produced remarkable quantities of free iodine. Bond's erstwhile challenger, *Southern Cross*, was unfortunately made of steel and the resultant chronic stress corrosion meant that one day the fancy steel rigging fell down on top of the crew. The indigenes were not unhappy when the Bondy fleet sailed for less unsympathetic waters, and left them to their lobster pots and fishing nets.

The Japanese have now moved into Yanchep in a big way, and are probably eating the seaweed and producing special reinforced iodine-resistant steel.

Twelve-metre racing is a relentless pursuit of excellence. It is based on interminable hours of sailing in all weather conditions, and the careful refining, honing and tuning of every possible variable. Sails are extremely expensive items, generally nowadays manufactured from Kevlar or Mylar, which, if not quite as light as gossamer, are certainly just as strong, if not stronger, than steel. After several outings the sails become so stretched and deformed as to be rendered useless. From the tender, one of the shore crew took photographs of the configuration of the trial-horse's spinnakers in various modes. These shots would subsequently be fed into computers to assess possible design improvements. At the end of a day's sailing, the sheds around Freo harbour buzz with the industry of sailmakers putting heavily analysed nips and tucks into genoas, spinnakers and mainsails. No such thing as an educated guess, and a quick session on the Singer. Thousands of pieces of data, carefully collected and collated, will determine even the slightest alteration.

We met *White Crusader*'s skipper, Harold Cudmore, on the harbour, after a hard three hours' sailing. He is a tall, wiry man, with thick, curly, auburn hair and aquiline features. He exudes a form of tireless, nervy energy which generates the impression that he is loathe to waste a single minute of his time in pointless endeavour. He was probably doing calisthenics as he talked to us.

Cudmore enjoys one of the highest of international reputations as a twelve-metre skipper. He is Irish, from Cork, and little is known about the man except that even Aeneas in his gutsier moments, or Jason and his Argonauts, had little on Harold.

I had heard on various occasions, and *always* from people who had never met the man, that he is an arrogant and awkward blighter. Not that I have anything against arrogant and awkward blighters. After all, I married one. But these are the sort of people who have never met Geoff Boycott, and will tell you exactly the same about him. Beware the received wisdom of hearsay, and the omniscient opinions of tabloid-informed twits!

Cudmore, in fact, could not have been more helpful, informative and charming. I mention his name in juxtaposition with that of Boycott, because there is an indefinable similarity between the two; perhaps it is the degree of concentration on the job to be done, which is often perceived by outsiders as stand-offish behaviour. Cudmore made it perfectly clear that he did not particularly want to talk to anybody until he had carried his sodden sails off board and back on shore. Only then was he ready for the fripperies of polite conversation. This, to my lights at least, is the focused sense of purpose of a true professional.

He showed us around the yachts, and adverted to the couple of hundred million things a skipper must keep his eye on whilst racing. From behind the helm, patently there is rather more to it than watching grass grow.

Quite apart from the America's Cup, the second Test at Perth has had plenty of competition for spectators this week. The mere sprinkling of folk on Sunday, the third day at the WACA, suggested that there was much better entertainment to be had elsewhere. Sure enough, Pope John Paul II, whose indefatigable peregrinations have added a new dimension to the concept of *urbi et orbi*, was winding up his six-day whistle-stop tour of Australia along the road at the Belmont Park Race Course, and causing the usual commotion.

By that stage in proceedings, the Australian team looked in dire need of some minor miracle of divine intervention beyond even the Pope's orchestration. The highlight of the English performance was, without doubt, a magnificent century by the gloriously 'in-nick' David Gower. (If, *on occasions*, this diary might *appear* totally, utterly and irretrievably biased in Fender's favour, it is because this diary *is* totally, utterly and irretrievably biased in Fender's favour.)

Rhodes scholar Prime Minister, Bob Hawke, no mean cricketer himself in his days up at Oxford, was much in evidence around the ground. There he was in the press box. There he was in the Channel 9 television commentary box. And there he was in the England and Australian dressing-rooms. Quite as ubiquitous as John Paul, really, but without the range of languages or the popular support.

Mr Hawke has organized a Prime Minister's XI versus an England XI one-day fixture in Canberra for 23 December, and patently did not see his selectorial remit confined to choosing his own team alone, and was making no secrets about the personalities he wanted to see gracing the opposition. No doubt apprised of superstars' sudden inexplicable attacks of non-specific back pain or unheralded hamstring trouble when similar fixtures occur so close to Christmas he was at great pains to mark the England line-up card. Meaningfully, he congratulated David Gower on his magnificent innings, and expressed a strong desire to see a similar performance in the Australian capital. 'And if *you* don't appear,' he explained, only half-jovially, to Ian Botham, 'you might have serious difficulty in getting a work permit for Queensland next year.'

Neither Ian Botham, however, nor for that matter the

disturbingly out-of-form Allan Lamb had managed to trouble the scorers in England's first innings that day. As penance, the pair of them shared a present Lamb's wife Lindsay had donated to England's Ashes effort. The gift caused great hilarity amongst the Perth crowd; to be worn affixed to the nose at all times by prime offenders, it was a bright orange/yellow duck's bill.

Meanwhile the greatest PR man on earth was entertaining a capacity crowd at the racecourse. Over 105,000 were in attendance, about one-tenth of the entire population of the Western Australian capital. People had queued all day just to catch a glimpse of the peripatetic Pontiff and, as happened in the USA, many appeared more interested in the package than in the product. Wild cheers, applause and acclaim greeted an extremely hard-line traditionalist sermon on the joy of vocations; on the ultimate gift to God of a priest or a nun in the family; on the evils of the materialistic consumer society. Swilling their tinnies and their stubbies in the bright sunshine, the crowd nodded their evil materialistic consumer approval.

This was the Pope's forty-second homily in six days, each one carefully prepared by the Pontiff himself during his annual holiday retreat in Castelgandolfo. There has been something for everyone. His strong appeal on Aboriginal land rights in Alice Springs constituted the emotional and political apogee of the tour, and ruffled not a few federal feathers. To give him due credit, this first non-Italian Pope for 450 years does not seem to care whether his message is popular or not. His stern moral views and traditionalism, his reactionary thinking on birth control and contraception, and his unassailable belief that the little woman is better off minding hearth and home, have alienated many Roman Catholics. After a decade's education in an Ursuline convent, I for example now find myself more or less lapsed. There is probably quite a large group of like-minded lapsers, who ought now to be constituting the bedrock of a modern, youthful Roman Catholic church, and who find themselves instead thus alienated. In retrospect, I fear that my particular form of education imbues adolescents with all the right principles, but then thrusts them, without relevant support structures, into a secular society where such principles, particularly on sex, are virtually impossible to abide by. What is even worse, for a lapsed Catholic, is that it is almost impossible to indulge in a good secular time without the subsequent remorse of a well-inculcated sense of guilt. 'Le sens du péché,' Baudelaire used to call it. You do exactly the same things as other less profoundly morally aware people, but, unlike them, you end up feeling very, very bad about it. It is a terrible thing, a Roman Catholic-framed conscience. I am sure such consciences inhabit some of the most deeply miserable creatures on earth.

There has been no shortage of more than gentle ironies to this papal visit. There has been much pontificating, for instance, on abject consumerism and soul-destroying materialism. Perhaps the message would have percolated through with greater spiritual purity if one of the visit's major sponsors had not been a South Australian beer company epitomizing both. And do not imagine for a moment that said brewery has not been getting its full PR mileage out of the fact! West End Export cans of beer are currently doing the rounds brightly decorated with a golden papal mitre. The marketing man's road to heaven is patently paved with empty tinnies.

There have also been quite a few benevolent pronouncements on the importance of a multi-cultural society, which coming from the leader of a church that has left no theological stone unturned in its rationale for wiping out entire, not sufficiently God-fearing cultures and societies in the past, have a tendency to sound somewhat risible. There have been cameos of the Pope kissing children, blessing old folk, hugging koala bears, wearing tin hats, going 'bush' and saying 'mate'. And there have been unholy seas of tasteless plastic souvenirs, fortunately the sort of thing for which the materialistic consumers do not mind shelling out a sponsoring bob or two. The sight of them brought back my childhood with a rush of melancholic nostalgia. In my early years, before I graduated to big-time materialistic consumerism, my most cherished possession had been a luminous glass bottle, cast in the presumed image and likeness of the Blessed Virgin Mary, and filled with holy water from the shrine at Lourdes by my favourite doting aunt, Margaret. Frankly, it beat rosary beads and pictures of stigmata-ridden saints hands down in entertainment value. From its centre-stage position on my dressing table, it used to glow with an unearthly luminescence in those twilight hours before I went to sleep. Like St Bernadette before me, I slumbered peacefully, dreaming of celestial visitations and waiting for the angels' voices which would come in useful during Mother Vianney's mental arithmetic tests.

Bored one day during the summer holidays with a replay of the entire Olympic Games against my three brothers (originally, as second eldest, I used to win the silver medal, but now the inexorable physical superiority of sex had superceded seniority, and I was edged off the medal list), I wandered around our light and airy house looking for some suitably stygian darkness in which to gaze at my incandescent Virgin. In my mother's dressing-room I remembered a large, free-standing wardrobe ideal for the purpose. I pushed my way in between the tightly packed dresses, skirts and blouses, and found myself in a deliciously tactile position smooched up against the mater's fur coat. I can still remember the sickening click as the wardrobe door closed shut behind me. The noxious smell of mothballs was overwhelming, and the stifling proximity of fur equally so. Our Lady of Lourdes shone beatifically in my frightened, clammy hand, but resolutely refused to perform any miracles.

I was hysterical. I banged on the door. The fur coat seemed to metamorphose into its original owner, and became decidedly aggressive. I fought it off. Empty wire coat hangers reproduced parthenogenetically, and conspired in clinking droves to enmesh me. Even at the tender age of seven, I could see that this would be a fairly ignominious way to go – smothered in a fur coat, strangled by a coat hanger.

The wardrobe eventually toppled over, presumably sending shock waves down the stair bannisters, across the hall, and into the kitchen, where dear old mum was imperturbably cooking dinner for twelve, annointing one brother with Dettol, strapping another up with Elastoplast, and keeping the third from pulverizing himself in the Magi-Mix. She raced upstairs, risking the distinct possibility of all three of them immediately sticking their heads in the gas oven. Rolling around in the dressing room she found a large mahogany wardrobe, temporarily inhabited by a petrified poltergeist, which she forthwith released, and exorcized with a swift clip across the ear.

To this day I remain frightened of the dark. When I think about it, I am sure that the only reason I married the dreaded P.H.E. was so that I need never be alone in the dark again. I had not counted on his becoming an international cricketer.

As a demonstration of the strengths of the human psyche, however, I am proud to relate that I *did* manage to overcome my paranoia of fur coats. And I still keep that bottle of Lourdes water.

The celebratory mass at the Belmont Park Race Course was nothing if not triumphalistic. The assembled crowd was treated, whilst waiting, to a repertoire of music conducted by former Professor of Music at the University of Western Australia, Sir Frank Calloway. The high note, if you will forgive the pun, was a fanfare, written by the late Master of the Queen's Music, Sir Arthur Bliss, and dedicated to Sir Frank on the occasion of Australia's last Commonwealth Games.

Unfortunately, the music for the Mass proper fell outside the mandate of the good professor, and we were served up something modern, complicated, contrapuntal and syncopated, the sort of thing that passes for trendy nowadays. It is odd, in a Church where the message is getting more reactionary by the minute, that the trammelling has become so do-or-die contemporary. Rather give me Brompton Oratory and some good Gregorian plain-chant any day of the week, and keep this cacophonic, atonal, arhythmic aural offensive for the popmongers.

In the Sacristy after the Mass, skippers and crew of challengers and defenders in the America's Cup lined up to meet the Pope. Perth entrepreneur Alan Bond, who embraced the faith when he married his wife Eileen, kissed the papal ring, the correct act of obeisance on such occasions, and was afterwards granted a special audience with John Paul. The roads were thronged with waving, excited people, perhaps half the population of Perth, as the Popemobile wended its way to the next and final Australian fixture, a nursing home run by nuns. 'G'day, Pope' proclaimed the quickly assembled placards. No insult intended, just the usual Aussie amalgam of good-natured, affectionate iconoclasm.

'And *whom* have you come to see?' I asked a six- or seven-year-old boy sporting a 'We love you, Pope' T-shirt, and a bright red be-mitred balloon. 'The Pope,' he answered correctly; 'he's come all the way from Italy, where my dad comes from.'

'And *why* has he come?' I continued, putting the poor youngster through an up-to-date catechism mill. 'He's come to make sure we keep the America's Cup, and to help us win the cricket,' he replied innocently, patently not a product of a Jesuit establishment. It makes you wonder, at the end of this brilliantly organized, media-oriented campaign, how much of the proverbial seed has actually fallen on good ground.

Back at the WACA, Australia were in deep trouble. Obdurately defensive captaincy from Mike Gatting, however, in failing to declare England's second innings at least an hour before the end of play on the fourth day, ensured a dogged draw.

A political scandal is currently causing the Government some little embarrassment. It's been a great year for political scandals and little embarrassments. First there was Oliver

North and Irangate, then Peter Wright and MI5, and now Paul Keating and the invisible tax returns. For a Treasurer, the poor man's memory would appear to contain more holes than a pair of tart's fishnet tights. Having initiated a national campaign to encourage, cajole and threaten the Australian taxpayer into filing his tax returns on time, a mysteriously mislaid Inland Revenue letter, which somehow found its way into the possession of the Leader of the Opposition, showed that the good Treasurer himself had not filed any tax returns for the previous two years. In the United Kingdom I am convinced the man would have been forced to resign; but Keating demonstrates a *mélange* of pained affront over his mail being tampered with, and a degree of political chutzpah which appears to have sidestepped the issue entirely. Australian politicians certainly seem better at brazening incidents out than most. Anyway, I merely mention this incident because Australia's pace hopes in this Test had rested fairly heavily on the veteran shoulders of injury-fraught Geoff Lawson. Lawson, sad to say, did not live up to expectation.

'Come on, Lawson,' remonstrated one less-than-sympathetic larrikin in the crowd, pyramid of empty Swan lagers at his side, nose glistening greasily from under the crushed-raspberry-coloured zinc cream. 'Come on, Lawson, you look about as fast as Keating's tax returns!'

The Australians were not the only cricketers copping flak, however. In the Channel 9 television commentary box, ex-England captain and erstwhile incomparable strategic genius, Bob Willis, was drawling away in his own inimitably soporific fashion. I am sure that PBL marketing, who package and sell cricket here in Australia on behalf of the less commercially minded Australian Cricket Board, could do a lot for Bob. If nothing else, they could market his dreary monologue laced with relentless inaccuracy as a non-proprietary alternative to Mogadon. In the England dressing-room, where everybody knows that Willis is in more danger of saying something original than of saying anything positive about Phil, the team was in fits. Left-arm spinner

Edmonds had picked up 2–50 while off-spinner Emburey had figures of about 1–100.

'But forget the figures,' droned Willis; 'you can see that Emburey has been by far the better bowler today.' On that particular day, frankly, informed opinion could not. Let us forget for a moment his totally incorrect assertions that the entire England team has sent me to Coventry over *Another Bloody Tour*, although they are conceivably actionable, causing me as they do such terrible mental distress. I just hope by now that any listeners automatically assume that anything Bob says about *la famille Edmonds* borders on being highly economical with the truth. Why on earth the Channel has not hired the mellifluous Welsh tones of the far more perceptive ex-England captain Tony Lewis instead is something I for one cannot fathom. I do believe I am not alone.

It was an eminently forgettable Test match, just the sort of game which reinforces the belief expressed by Western Australian and Australian left-arm pace man, Chris Matthews. He went on record as saying that he found cricket a boring game to watch. If the players themselves find it boring, what hope is there for the rest of us?

Not, of course, that I spent much time in physical propinquity to the ground. There was too much going on that week to take time out watching run-choked draws at the WACA. The day before the start of the Test, I had been prevailed upon to address the Western Australian section of the Lord's Taverners. In England, the Taverners do a lot of good work for handicapped kids, but in Australia their efforts are focused more on providing sporting facilities for children in need.

Prior to my departure a few telexes had arrived in London from honorary secretary Harry Sorenson, inquiring whether I would care to be the first woman ever to make the keynote speech at a Lord's Taverners' thrash in Australia. These telexes I studiously ignored, much as Phil and Paul Keating do income-tax returns, hoping that in the fullness of time they would merely fade away. Mr Sorenson, however, is more tenacious than that. I met him on our first trip to Perth for the State match, at a Lord's Taverners' cocktail party thrown in honour of the two teams. Malleably good-natured as I am, after two flûtes of Moët I had acceded to his request. I woke up the next morning, as ladies often do after New Year's Eve parties, wondering what on earth had possessed me to say 'yes'. I had done quite a bit of public speaking at school and, for want of competition, even won the odd English-Speaking Union award. There had been no choice in the matter. Being embarrassingly useless at games of all sorts in those less than halcyon convent days, the majority of my leisure time had had to be spent in more satisfyingly vocal pursuits. Whilst my Amazonian contemporaries thwacked hell out of one another on the lacrosse field, and bashed one another's shins black and blue with ladylike dexterity on the hockey pitch, I wimped out unobtrusively into extra drama, singing, and public speaking lessons. I had extra piano lessons, too, although they were more of a penance. Mother Benigna would rap me painfully over the knuckles for imperfect renditions of mindlessly repetitive arpeggios, whilst the acme of my musical aspiration was simply to bang out bad boogey, hard honky-tonk and passably simplified imitations of Burt Bacharach.

I had spoken a few times at the Cambridge Union, too, deliberately fatuous and apolitical stuff whilst my meaningful left-wing peers were all but throwing themselves under steam-rollers over American involvement in Vietnam, or whatever the in outrage-of-the-day was at that time. Now, after a decade of public-speaking silence, I was on the podium again for a thirty-minute speech.

A greater than normal percentage of ladies turned up for the lunch at a major international Perth hotel, where over 350 people assembled to hear the life story of the beast of burden that is the professional cricket widow. It was reassuring to see Mrs Ian Chappell, Mrs Rod Marsh and Mrs Greg Shippard attending in kindly supportive sorority. A reporter from London's *Sun* was also in evidence, presumably to see if any aggro of the pink-gin-swilling-dodderers variety could be created out of this, another *private* fund-raising function.

It is true that there were people rolling around in the aisles, but whether this was due to my often misunderstood sense of humour, or to violent attacks of gastro-enteritis from the inevitable prawn cocktail, was not entirely apparent. The speech revolved around life with PHE and the difficulties of living with a character who must be the world's most unhandy man. There was the episode when I came home from a conference in Brussels, and found that he had been having a go at Do It Yourself. I walked into the bedroom, and there over the Edmonds' connubial couch was a mirror perilously affixed to the ceiling.

'What's this for,' I asked, 'so I can watch myself having a headache?'

'The trouble with you, Frances,' Phil retorted, 'is that I cannot remember the last time you said you enjoyed having sex.'

'Why should you?' I replied. 'You weren't there.'

It was all in a good cause.

The next morning was a very early start. Doing guest spots for the Sydney-based breakfast television show *Good Morning, Australia* generally involves getting up fairly early, but this was ridiculous. Since Perth is three hours behind Sydney, we went on air at 4.30 a.m., which involved getting up at 3 a.m. I wandered around the vast lobby of the Merlin at 3.45 a.m., waiting for the taxi to arrive. The night staff gave me some unashamedly funny looks. All tarted up, with full television screen make-up, waiting for a taxi at 3.45 in the morning. I must have looked like somebody's discarded hooker.

The one good thing about doing breakfast TV is that it does leave you the rest of the day free to feel absolutely knackered. I am beginning to feel, in a minor sort of way, how Selina Scott must have felt after a couple of years of this routine.

The phone was ringing as I returned to the sordid sanctuary of our hotel room. The collection of cricket kit, clothes, memorabilia, books, 'gimmies', toiletries, rancid laundry bags, coffins, computers, word-processors, executive toys, electronic chess, papers, silly hats, bottles of Johnnie Walker whisky, and half-used tubes of sun screen has now reached disturbingly seedy hazard proportions. One hotel room does not accommodate two Edmondses. Phil, heaving like a beached whale in between the Janet Reger, could not quite bestir himself to answer the call. It is interesting how a man who can happily wake me up at 4 a.m. with the World Service, whenever possible is resolutely comatose until 9 a.m. should I be obliged to make an early start. The call was from Alan Bond's personal assistant, David Michael. Did I want to go out sailing that day with Eileen Bond?

Did I want to go out sailing with the legendary 'Red' Bond? Do fish swim? Is the Pope Catholic? Do David Gower and Frances Edmonds indulge in the odd glass of Bollinger? Does Dolly Parton sleep on her back?

Sailing with Eileen is about as far removed from the twelve-metre concept of the sport as you can get. Sailing with Eileen does not mean winch-grinding, or sail trimming or tacking, or anything in any way remotely strenuous. Sailing with Eileen means boarding one of the sumptuous Bondy cruisers (that day we sailed on *Southern Cross II;* the mega-million dollar *Southern Cross III*, just purchased, was still being fitted out), rocking forth comfortably to the starting line, maintaining spirits high with anything from bottles of vintage Dom Perignon to tinnies of the company product, as Eileen calls the Bond-produced Swan Lager, taking a brief respite with an oyster-and-crayfish lunch, and returning replete to the Dom or the company product to watch the sequence of events. It is a splendid way to watch other poor blighters throwing thirty-odd tacks, and breaking their backs sailing a twelve-metre in a thirty-knot wind.

Eileen is great fun, the warm and generous household power behind the Bondy throne. Married to Alan when they were both teenagers, she still takes a keen interest in the manifold ramifications of the enormous Bond empire, and pointed with obvious pride to the Observation City Hotel, which the Bonds had built to accommodate the hoped-for influx of tourist for the America's Cup. Eileen, who runs her own successful interior design company, had organized the décor for the entire place and the tropical swimming pool has to be seen to be believed. Looking out over the Indian Ocean, with peerless views of the racing, Observation City must surely be the place to stay at the moment.

I took to her immediately. I like any woman who has a reputation for being a legend in her own lunchtime, will sing Irish songs where and when she feels like it and remains resolutely herself. She has a shock of flaming red hair, hence the nickname, a heart of gold and a couple of kilos of diamonds liberally distributed over her person.

'Well, Alan owns the mine. Why shouldn't I wear the diamonds?' she asks. Truly a woman after my own heart.

Some of the less flamboyant, more conservative, perhaps even envious elements of Perth society dismiss the Bonds as 'new money'. Bond answers such sniping by pointing out that he made his first million by the time he was twenty. Now nearing the half-century mark, he reckons that makes him an old millionaire. Besides, as Nancy Reagan is apocryphally credited with saying: 'Better *nouveau riche* than not *riche* at all.'

That day the Bond syndicate's *Australia IV* was sailing against Syd Fischer's *Steak 'n' Kidney*. Sadly for us, the Sydney yacht was leading by quite a substantial margin. Spirits aboard *Southern Cross II* became proportionately lower. Jody, Eileen's youngest daughter, went downstairs to watch the television in sheer frustration and despair. All of a sudden I remembered that I had been awake since some ungodly hour, and felt overwhelmingly tired. I asked our hostess whether she minded if I took a quick nap. There were, after all, three magnificently appointed state-rooms with *en suite* bathrooms on board.

'You just go into my bedroom and lie down,' said Eileen, concerned; 'and make sure you cover yourself up. If there's anything you want, you just phone upstairs.'

Eileen Bond is clearly first and foremost an extremely soft-touch mother.

By the time I woke up, the celebrations were in full flow. One of *Steak 'n' Kidney*'s sails had become entangled in the rudder, and *Australia IV* had romped home victorious.

Eileen, in a wonderful choice of culinary metaphor, was devouring a steak and kidney pie. She was in fine fettle.

'I bet Syd Fischer wishes he had kissed the Pope's ring,' she laughed.

She admits to being a tiny bit superstitious. During the final round against the New York Yacht Club in Newport, she had been wearing a jumper when *Australia II* won its first race against Dennis Conner's *Liberty*. It was a bulky knit job, with a fur koala bear appliquéd up a gum tree on the front. She kept on wearing it, laundering it in the evening, and wearing it again the next day until *Australia II* had won the Cup. Forget Ben Lexcen's radical winged keel, and John Bertrand's seamanship. Not many people realize that it was Red's jumper that secured the Auld Mug for the Aussies.

Unfortunately, our mates on *White Crusader* had had a bad day, vanquished by *French Kiss* after trouble with their sails. It is such a dicey business, this twelve-metre sailing lark. There are so many variables, vagaries and vicissitudes to cope with, apart from the already complicated business of plain sailing.

'We'll have lunch next time you come to Perth,' said Eileen, handing me her address and telephone number as we moored. I would have to put some practice in on the Irish ballads.

Phil arrived home in a foul mood, berating everyone and as usual muttering darkly about 'negative fucking tactics'. He lay on the bed zapping from TV station to TV station. I think remote-control devices should be banned from all households comprised of more than one person. They are the most anti-social invention since garlic capsules.

It is perhaps a hallmark of Western civilization that we all need space. Space to sit in, space to move in, space to live in. On my flight to Australia, I sat next to a beautiful petite Malaysian lady. From her perfect poise throughout the twenty-four hour flight, it was perfectly obvious that the space afforded by a club-class seat would have been more than enough for her to set up house in. Whilst I tried every possible angle and posture in increasingly redundant efforts to doze, she just folded up as neatly as a pac-a-mac and went to sleep for hours. But I am, unfortunately, a real Westerner and living in the close physical proximity of a small hotel room with one large cricketer for months on end is becoming a bit of a trial. Different circadian rhythms, the fact that I want to work when he wants to watch the dot on the television screen once all the broadcasts have finished, all these problems, which are in no way so acute in normal living quarters, become further and further exacerbated in a rabbit-hutch environment. It is also very difficult to write if there is a bed in the immediate vicinity. The tendency is to lie on it and the inevitable kip ensues. But that is my own specific problem. I am merely beginning to realize, albeit in a luxurious sort of way, that a lack of living space must engender aggression and, on a large scale, intense social strife; what our urban developers often forget is that most people prefer their relatively spacious slums to an all-mod-con, no social nexus, high-rise box.

Being in such a negative fucking frame of mind himself, old Edmonds decided that he no longer wanted to go to the Elton John concert that evening. Elton is doing one of his show-stopping tours here in Australia, complete with the entire Melbourne Symphony Orchestra, and has invited the team to any one of his three performances in Perth. He certainly loves his cricket, Elton, and according to Phil talks knowledgeably even on the finest subtleties of the game. It was just too bad that we missed that concert. We went along the next night only to find that the performance had been cancelled. Unsubstantiated rumours abounded amongst the bitterly disappointed fans that Elton had been out that afternoon on a businessman's yacht, and ended up well and truly ratted. Although that seemed – to me at least – like an eminently more sensible way for a superstar to be spending his time, the bad-mouthers were shamefacedly obliged to eat their words some weeks later, when their hero was taken into a Sydney hospital for throat surgery. Two nights later the two cricket teams were invited by the West Australian Trotting Association to the trotting races.

I had never been to the trotting before, and therefore hid the TV remote control from Phil in an effort to encourage him to come along. It was, however, the fact that we bumped into some whizz-kids out from the City of London to advise the Bond Corporation which tipped Phil's scales. They too had been invited, thanks to Swan Lager's sponsorship of the sport, and so we all set off together.

Received wisdom has it that Australian trotting is irredeemably rigged. Don't believe a word of it! My card was 'marked' by one of the sponsors putatively in the know. It may well have been that the gentleman in question was a numerical dyslexic, but suffice it to say that I won not one by now fairly worthless Australian dollar. Indeed, I would have done far better to follow my original instincts and stick to cricket-related horses:

'It's Simply Magic' . . . David Gower in his magnificent first-innings century knock.

'Careless Hands' . . . fluffed chances by Boon, Border, Ritchie *et al* during England's first innings.

'King Command' . . . England manager, Peter Lush.

'Jester Boy' . . . Allan Lamb complete with duck's bill.

'Astonishment' . . . general sensation in hitherto excoriating British press corps.

'Lord Cognac' . . . Phil Edmonds, whose celebrated connections with Hine keep the team's spirits up.

'Bonnie Skipper' . . . Mike 'pass me the cheese-and-pickle sandwiches' Gatting.

'Super Force',⎫
'Star Rogue' ⎬ . . . controversial hard-hitter Ian Botham.

'Little Napoleon' . . . assistant manager and disciplinarian Micky Stewart, also known as 'Sieg Heil'.

'Two Thousand Extra' . . . Man of the Match award worth $2,000, which went to English opening batsman Chris Broad.

'Fiery Black' . . . Barbados-born Gladstone Small.

'General Alert' . . . situation in the Australian Cricket Board.

'Another Dustbin' . . . present resting-place of Australian selectors' current policy.

It would be difficult to claim, in all honesty, that the trotting was cosmically interesting. The company, on the contrary, genuinely was. I have never been 'money-literate' and was intrigued to hear how naughty boys in the City, and indeed all over the world, 'ramp' shares. They all get together over the international blower in the morning and decide that they will move into a particular share. Because so many people are then buying that share, the market perceives an interest, and your average punter will therefore move in too, further hiking the price. Eventually the boys get out fast at an enormous paper profit, and the schmucks like you and me are left with shares which plummet overnight. In Perth alone, for example, millions of dollars have been made overnight ramping shares. The stock is usually highly speculative and, as the saying goes in Western Australia, 'many a good share has been ruined by drilling the mine'. It is all a question of confidence, expectation and a goodly amount of the average punter's wholesome greed. It's comforting to know that there's a quicker way of making a quid than interminable hours at the tripe-writer.

A most welcome surprise awaited us on our return to the hotel. During a radio interview with Philip Satchell, on the ABC in Adelaide, the conversation had inevitably turned to Australian wines and the ersatz champagnes or sparkling white wines produced here which, on the whole, are remarkably potable and extremely reasonable brews.

Robert Mayne, the group public-relations manager of Thomas Hardy and Sons, famed South Australian wine-makers, had therefore sent me a bottle of Hardy's Classique Cuvée of excellent 1981 vintage, and invited me down to Reynella when we arrived in Adelaide for the third Test. I drank the bottle of bubbly with All-Sport photographer, Adrian Murrell, and we both agreed over our Chinese meal that it was decidedly superior to any non-vintage French stuff. Poor Adrian. He had been so bored during the last day's play at the WACA that he had fallen asleep and missed every dismissal. And this is a man who earns his living taking photographs of cricket! Perhaps that more than anything bore eloquent testimony to the tedium which that second Test in Perth had generated.

6

The Big Sleep
and then Adelaide

The England team is back in form again. Men who would
kill to play in a Test match are often suddenly laid low
when it comes to playing a State match in front of the
proverbial two men and a dog, or, with deference to our
Australian hosts at the Melbourne Cricket Ground, two
men and a dingo.

Our beloved Scottish physiotherapist Lawrie 'MacDuff'
Brown currently has his hands full with Test stars unavail-
able to play in the Sir Robert Menzies Memorial match.
Paceman Graham Dilley is out with fluid on the right knee.
All-rounder Phillip DeFreitas is out with a jarred knee. Ian
'Living Legend' Botham is out with a seriously strained
muscle in his left side. And off-spinner John Emburey
is out with the hitherto unchronicled in Gray's *Anatomy*
complaint of a Melbourne-based wife and two children.

This leaves England with a somewhat depleted attack of
three specialist bowlers: Neil 'Ever enthusiastic' Foster;
Gladstone 'Out to prove himself' Small; and Phil 'I've got
two cracked fingers, but there is nobody else left is there?'
Edmonds.

'The medium pace of captain Mike Gatting will be used
in support, along with occasional off-spin from Surrey's

Jack Richards,' came the official management explanation. Richards, who must have bowled all of at least a dozen overs in first-class cricket, was no doubt relieved to learn that he was not expected simultaneously to keep wicket as well. Given the paucity of the willing and able, the sidelined glove man, constantly cheerful Bruce French, was to be given his first chance behind the stumps in weeks.

Frankly, the whole business was such a shambles, it could have been an amalgam of *Emergency Ward 10* and *Fawlty Towers*, with manager Peter Lush doing a very good Basil in his obfuscations to the press about what had happened, what was happening and, *a fortiori*, what was about to happen.

Our present sojourn is the recently renovated Menzies at Rialto Hotel and, according to the blurb, the Rialto next door is the tallest structure in the southern hemisphere. Not a lot of people know that. 'What is the tallest building in the southern hemisphere?' they will Trivially Pursue you one day at the WI coffee morning. 'The Rialto building in Melbourne,' you will respond, with the speed of an IBM number-cruncher.

The edifice is based on a laudable architectural concept. The old façade and turrets have been carefully preserved, and a dozen floors of iron-balustraded bedroom corridors look down on to a communal cobbled courtyard. The effect is very much that of the HM prison depicted in the ever popular Ronnie Barker television series, *Porridge*. Wags ever mindful of alleged torrid nights in the Caribbean were not slow to suggest that the hotel had been selected on purpose, so that disciplinarian Micky 'Warden Mackay' Stewart could lock the lads in at night.

For once, locking the team in at night was not the problem. Getting them up in the morning, however, apparently was. This was to be the day when not only were early spectators at the Sir Robert Menzies Memorial Match confronted with a half-strength England side but, worse, their captain Mike Gatting failed to turn up at all.

It would, of course, be heartening to relate that the press

box was electric with a sense of righteous outrage. The atmosphere in the press box was certainly electric, but more with the unconnected word-processor wires of those multifarious correspondents who would rock in around lunchtime. The only righteous outrage was being demonstrated quite vociferously by yours truly (whom yet another obstructive little minion was trying to debar from her rightful position in the press box), and by the half-dozen journos who had actually made it in time for the start of play.

One of the team, and few they were who were not either physically on the field or pretending to be paraplegic until they attacked the golf course later that day, was despatched to locate the captain, who was assumed to be in his cabin and a thousand miles away. His telephone was, unfortunately, off the hook, and the emissary failed to rouse him with ear-piercing rings on the door bell, and elephantine thumps on the door. It was all quite a mystery to many of us. Apart from anything, nobody had ever imagined that Gatt could manage to exist for more than two consecutive hours without solid food. Ever imaginative, however, members of the press corps came up with the answer. He must have found a way of eating without waking up.

Now, whatever David Gower's faults and failings as captain in the West Indies, it is nevertheless a matter of fact that even he realized State matches were not optional. Practice nets, yes. But State matches, never. Exactly what the press and P. B. H. May would have organized for old Fender had he missed the start of a game defies contemplation. Crucifixion would not have been out of the question. I also remember when Phil was once five minutes late, not for the start of play at Middlesex, but five minutes after the appointed time to be at the ground, which was an hour and a half before the start of play. In fact, Phil was not even late at all. He had turned up early, and then gone to leave some tickets at the gate. Middlesex captain Gatting and vice-captain John Emburey both saw to it that Phil was to be banned from the match, and from the two subsequent ones. This was all a few weeks before the England team for India was due to be selected, and with Phil trying to live down a reputation as an awkward tourist. In fact I actually took Gatt to task over the incident last year in Trinidad, and he countered that at that time Phil had not been giving him the support he needed. That, quite frankly, was an interesting analysis. Perhaps the person who had given Gatt the hardest time in his embryonic captaincy had been John Emburey, relieved of the job that would have been his, had he not cleared off on a rebel South African tour the day after he attended a Middlesex Committee meeting, yet failed to mention the fact. The truth of the matter was that that particular season only one bowler had been getting any wickets for Middlesex, and it was P. H. E. And it was also, ironically, P.H.E. who on this occasion argued strenuously against the calls for harsh censure of Gatt.

Meanwhile, back in the dressing-room, Mike Gatting had still failed to materialize, though there would be quite an amount of material when he did. It had fallen, therefore, to the oldest member of the team, Philippe-Henri, to give the pre-match pep-talk to this hardly more than demi-team.

'No!' interrupted someone at one juncture. 'No, that won't do. That's a three-syllable word and Gatt doesn't know any three-syllable words.'

'Oh, yes he does,' countered wicket-keeper-suddenly-elevated-to-relief-bowler Jack Richards, mindful of the skipper's increasingly generous girth. 'Ham-burg-er.'

Talking of food, I had lunch that day in one of those splendidly appointed function-rooms at the MCG with the Lady Mayoress and her fund-raising committee. Christmas and Christmas-related fund-raising charities are in the air, although it seems odd to someone used to northern hemisphere conditions when Christmas precursors are being played out in thirty-degree temperatures. All over Australia, shopping malls are full of artificial, polystyrene-based snow, and Father Christmas sledges being drawn by white kangaroos, a geographical variation on the original theme. In Melbourne, however, there is an even more interesting departure from tradition. You'd better believe it! A *Mother* Christmas. And not just one. Several. I asked the Lady Mayoress what it could all mean, and she explained that the Women's Equal Opportunities lobby had insisted on it. If you are going to have a father, they argued, then you have got to have a mother. This has now caused further ructions with the one-parent family lobby, who obviously believe otherwise. The season of peace and goodwill towards all men is indeed fraught with tension.

The great lie-in was, if nothing else, an astounding tribute to the public relations skills of manager Peter Lush. (As good old Engel pointed out, rather an unfortunate surname for a team with England's alleged drinking habits.) If only Lushy had been there to deal with the alleged broken beds in Barbados, I am perfectly persuaded that the hotel in question would have ended up paying Botham compensation for any discomfort or embarrassment caused. Within twenty-four hours the entire sleepy Gatting incident had been relegated to the jokes department, rather than being allowed to lead to calls for resignation. Gatting was not even fined by the management, a piece of excessive forbearance with the blue-eyed boy which most correspondents thought quite wrong. It looks as if winning even a single bloody Test match for England means *carte blanche* from now on.

Preparations are already under way for the Christmas Party we shall be celebrating on our return to Melbourne for the Fourth Test. Each member of the team has been issued with a letter of the alphabet, and must dress accordingly, taking the theme from that letter. This year, for the first time ever, wives, and not only wives but children and nannies, will also be allowed to participate in the festivities. This is yet another indication of Lush's unfailing common sense. Splitting couples up on Christmas Day has been a stupidly divisive ploy on previous tours, and has only led to much merry festal post-prandial aggro.

Phil and I have been awarded the letter J. Inspired by the prison-like configuration of the Menzies, we thought we would go along as Jail-birds, and went accordingly to a fancy-dress shop to hire our convict outfits for the big event.

'Don't know why you bother,' remarked Engel laconically. 'With the letter J you could just put a towel around your waist, and go as Joan Jones' (see p. 16).

I had lunch that week with my Heinemann moles, who were full of great *non sub judice* anecdotes about the MI5 trial, and with Somerset captain Peter Roebuck. 'Prof', as the latter is called at Somerset (after all, the dear boy did gain a First in Law at Cambridge), is not entirely disinterested in the proceedings himself. After the jolly Somerset County Cricket Club eviscerations, which ended in the dismissal of West Indians Viv Richards and Joel Garner, and the consequent resignation of Ian Botham, Peter's recently published book, *It Sort of Clicks (Ian Botham talking to Peter Roebuck)* is destined to become a collector's item. Botham does not, it would appear, do too much talking to him now.

No matter, Peter's talents are currently deployed on another book, this time a far more worthwhile pursuit than the old ghosted biography guff. Why any near-genius should waste his time and literary efforts in making dumbos look bright, and thickos appear interesting, is beyond me anyway. This time Peter has drawn inspiration from a far more eminent source, the celebrated Australian poet Henry Lawson, and a piece from the anthology *The Land where Sport is Sacred* has provided his next title, *Heroes and Clods* (though I know his publisher prefers *Ashes to Ashes*).

Try as I would, Peter was not being drawn on who was going to be categorized where.

The moles were in good form, recounting tales true and apocryphal of the Sir Robert Armstrong meets Malcolm Turnbull confrontation. It sounded like the slaughter of the innocents, although on reflection a British cabinet secretary would most probably have avoided slaughter on that count. Turnbull, of course, is the stiletto-sharp Sydney boy turned Rhodes Scholar at Oxford who cut his teeth on the Test and County Cricket Board in the early days of Kerry Packer's World Series Cricket. Then, the TCCB had placed excessively punitive restrictions on the Packer rebels, and ended up, thanks to Malcolm, paying out vast amounts of compensation for restraint of trade. Since then, Malcolm has gone from strength to strength, and the urbane, polished, charming and discreet Sir Robert (at least, when he is not 'jostling' photographers at Heathrow) has more than met his match. Turnbull's is a relentlessly needling and irreverent approach . . . 'Mr Armstrong – oh, I'm sorry . . . I'm a closet Republican, you know . . . Sir Robert . . .'

Apart from the fact that the poor man had the job of being economical with the truth on behalf of the British Government, and was constantly obliged to obfuscate quite blatantly, it was unfortunate for Sir Robert that he should one day have embarked on some abstruse point about 'sophistication'. The ensuing dialogue, *non expressis verbis*, went something like this:

'I see,' said Malcolm, sensing the wily old trout on the end of his line, and about to reel him in:

'I see. So let us, Sir Robert, define sophistication. I suppose you, Sir Robert, would define yourself as sophisticated?'

Sir Robert nodded his head with all the *gravitas* of a Whitehall mandarin.

'And I, I as another fellow Oxford graduate, I suppose I could be defined as sophisticated, too?' hypothesized Malcolm.

Again, Sir Robert concurred, with a more grudging inclination of the head.

'So *you* as an Oxford graduate, and *I* as an Oxford graduate, *we* could both be defined as sophisticated?' asked Malcolm, who has clearly also attended a Berlitz school of advocacy.

'Yes,' agreed Sir Robert.

'Only difference being,' added Malcolm, landing his prey after a few minutes' teasing, 'that I got a First.'

Whether these stories be true or false, they certainly make highly entertaining reading for the Pom-bashing Aussies, and for anyone who believes that the Armstrongs of life are professionally inimical to 'open government', and it is good to have them rumbled on occasion.

Somewhat less entertaining, however, was the break-in at the Heinemann premises in Melbourne, soon after the Wright manuscript had been delivered, when files were stolen and the safe tampered with. It would, of course, be nothing but circumstantial to attribute the attempted larceny to British security forces, but educated MI5/MI6 watchers felt that the degree of incompetent cock-up displayed seemed disturbingly liable to indicate just them. In the meantime, the irrepressible Tam Dalyell, he of *Belgrano* notoriety, has again been asking embarrassing questions on the floor of the House at Westminster.

The circus is on the move again, back to Adelaide for the third Test. The hostess on our flight suggested over the intercom system that passengers should moderate their voices, as Mr Gatting was trying to get some sleep. People read and people dozed. Our three English-West Indians, Gladstone Small, Phillip DeFreitas and Wilf Slack, affectionately known as the 'Three Degrees', played cards. Graham Dilley, ever petrified of flying, sat as usual with his Walkman firmly affixed to his head, clenched knuckles white with panic. Peter Lush, none too impressed with flying, either, walked up and down the plane, chatting amicably. Allan Lamb, relentlessly mischievous, was busily squirting magic ink on whomsoever should cross his path. One wretched and overworked air hostess was less than impressed when a large, black blob was splashed across the front of her blouse, but was confused when it faded to invisibility before she could enjoin the captain to have Lambie thrown off the plane. We all ate the in-flight plastic airline food which none of us really wanted, and wondered why. In short it was the usual team transfer.

Next day, Phil and I went off to visit Hardy's Winery at Reynella, with Jack and Birjitta Richards. Birjitta has been with the tour since Newcastle, and is such a welcome addition to any party. She is Dutch, with that thick, curly blonde hair, pretty face and faultless complexion which so epitomizes the beauties of that nation. Despite all that, I cannot help but like her. Both she and Jack were apparently astounded when he was selected for the tour, and Jack's projected plans to become an optician have had to be put on the optical back burner for the time being. Birjitta too is working hard in preparation for a business-studies course back home in England. It is a great, albeit dog-in-a-manger comfort to know that when I am hard at it whilst the other girls are soaking up the rays on the beach, Birjitta is also swotting away somewhere down the team corridor.

Most of the wives and loved ones are out here by now. My partner in many a giddy caper, Mrs Lindsay Lamb, has been keeping us all amused, especially with her exhibition of Olympic dressage skills on the pedigree horse. Romany Foster, another inmate of the 'Not the Team Room' I arranged for the girls last year in Barbados, and a dab hand with the rum punches and the banana daiquiris, arrived in Melbourne. The Botham family have flown out, complete with nanny. The Emburey family is here, with two children. Janet Athey, a bright, French-speaking lady, who flies with Air France, joined us in Adelaide. Ellen French is also here, with the children, and Gladstone Small's Australian fiancée, Lois, is with us, too, a real fun-loving, bubbly character. She would have to be. She told me that her Perth-based parents had been obliged to change their telephone number after a series of obscene and obnoxious calls subsequent to a picture of herself and West Indian-born Gladstone appearing in the local rag. We both tried flippantly to make light of the incident, dispensing with Aussies in general, and Western Australians in particular, as a crowd of xenophobic racists. Exaggerated though such statements patently are, they are unfortunately not quite as far from the truth as one would like to believe. It certainly seems that Australians are far more ethnocentric than we are in the United Kingdom, and doubtless the poorer for it.

The Hardy's Winery folk invited me to the South Australian Winemakers versus 'Press' cocktail competition the following day, as honorary captain of the McLaren Vale team. It was certainly a more interesting and enriching experience than the repeat tedium of the Test match trundling along down the road at the Adelaide Oval. You know full well, when you start reading regular cricket correspondents making much of 'an interesting day', 'an intriguing session' or, worse still, 'a match pregnant with possibilities', that you have probably been watching the dreariest cricket that folk have been subjected to for some time. The protracted ennui of the second Test in Perth was bad enough, but Adelaide took the proverbial boredom biscuit. The impeccable batting track at the Oval was certainly a credit to its curator, Les Burdett, but from the rain-affected outset it was clear that a draw was inevitable. Burdett, incidentally, is the groundsman who has long criticized batsmen's use of rubber-soled shoes, the infamous 'nipples', and maintains that the less popular spikes aerate the pitch rather than merely tear off the top-grass, whilst also giving the spin bowlers some rough to bowl at on the fourth and fifth days. Burdett has produced such perfect pitches that his argument is gaining currency, and spikes are now mandatory in Sheffield Shield matches at the Oval. The message is now being preached for Test matches, too.

The ground (should one even dare suggest such a thing?) was perhaps even too perfect, too good a batting track for both sides for a result to be possible. A lady spectator even produced an ironing board at one stage, plugged the Rowenta into an outside-broadcasting van, and started to do the week's ironing!

Down at the cocktail competition, things were very different. Our concoction, entered under the appellation of 'Foxy Fizz', was subtitled 'Irridescent Mediocrity', an expression which had crossed my mind whilst watching the England and Australian teams staggering along sluggishly at the Oval. Conceived and created by Hardy's chief wine-maker, Geoff Weaver, group PR manager, Robert Mayne and *moi-même*, it featured a mystery aphrodisiac, which one judge decided was the ephemeral taste of fox piss. It was in fact a fine, complex, delicate blend of gin, méthode champenoise, sparkling white wine and exotic tropical fruits. The nose was dominated by lifted amyl acetate and lemon, while its palate had a balance of sugar, acid and alcohol, rare in its subtle nuances. This was a cocktail to be drunk immediately, to be kept for several minutes, or to be chundered within the hour. It was a cocktail to reward the patient, and true connoisseurs would note the juniper berry backbone.

There were various other cocktails on offer. 'The Papal Cocktail' – one slug and you fall flat on your face and kiss the ground; 'Acid Test'; 'Mouldy Bubbles'; 'Boo Lagoon'; and 'Passionate Plunge'. The winner was fielded by the opposition. 'The Presstitutes', who came up with 'Rupert's Revenge'. Whether or not this was a subtle reference to Rupert Murdoch's current designs to win back his lost birthright, the *Herald and Weekly Times*, was unclear. At all events it was a very professional effort, sugar on the outer rim, but a fierce punch locked in the complicated and sophisticated mixture below. Nobody, and certainly not the Presstitutes, was admitting to any metaphors.

Five consecutive days on a featherbed pitch was taking its toll on the bowlers. Phil and Embers certainly toiled away for an England team suffering from the loss of Ian Botham, still unfit with a strained intercostal muscle. Phil, too, had sustained a strained intercostal muscle, contracted from reading a report in a copy of the *Zimbabwe Herald*. A Muzarabani housewife, it ran, was shot dead by her husband when he woke in the middle of the night and mistook her for a wild pig. I thought the report was moderately funny, but for some reason Phil found it hysterically so. The piece, sadly in both our views, did not include a photo of the lady concerned.

The Test ended up as another drearily depressing draw,

and it seems perhaps high time that PBL marketing reworked some of its hyperbolic advertising slogans. Television slots featuring a lion and a kangaroo in dramatic and exciting 'Clashes for the Ashes' are perhaps a trifle over-the-top even by PR standards. Certainly the radio publicity, boasting of the Australian team going lion-catching, has lost a degree of its street cred, if ever it had any to begin with. It is unlikely on current form that such claims will see out the last two Tests.

Indeed, the deprecating humour now focused on the hapless Aussies is more than vaguely reminiscent of England's unhappier days last year in the Windies. Former Australian skipper and leg-spinner Richie Benaud has just come up with a revolutionary new practice method to improve the leg-spin of Peter Sleep, and the off-spin of Greg Matthews. These two were expected to play a major role in Australia's bowling attack in the third Test, and in an effort to give them a mental picture of a perfect line and length, Richie took the pair off to the nets and obliged them to bowl with their eyes closed. Wags in the England team declared that they thought the Australian opening attack had already been doing just that, in Perth.

The rain came and, all in all, it was a fairly dismal display. Just a fortnight prior, a freak storm of mini-cyclone proportions had swept through the Oval, taking the roof off the stand and leaving a huge girder deposited like a Zeus-hurled thunderbolt in the middle of the pitch. Unfortunately, nothing quite so theatrical happened during the game, as the two teams went through the redundant motions. Entertainment rating of the third Test . . . nil.

Far more fun, in fact, was to be had elsewhere at, of all places, the Payneham City Library, where I ended up one day for a book-signing session. As is the case in England, libraries in Australia are shamefully under-utilized, except by elderly folk, who often come along for the community atmosphere, and by hidebound young mothers who know they can grab a few minutes' respite by lobbing the little ankle-biters for half an hour into the crêche provided.

In Adelaide some radical thinking had been devoted to ways of attracting youngsters along to the library to teach them how to use the institution, to locate a book and to learn how to enjoy the fading art of reading. So many children nowadays are brought up in the world of passive entertainment, processed and packaged for them on the dreaded box, or in the higher-technology world of mindlessly repetitive computer games. Such developments indicate that the art of reading may well end up severely jeopardized.

And it came to pass that one of the libraries devised a 'Chuck a Barbara Cartland' competition. The idea was self-evident. Children were simply encouraged to chuck a tome of the works of that queen of schmaltz as far as possible. The sheer impertinence of the game created absolute furore amongst many of the more narrow-minded citizens of Adelaide, but others felt that it was the best thing suggestible adolescents could possibly do with such volumes. The number of sentimental ladies who have had their expectations raised, their brains addled and their grasp on reality undermined by such cloud-cuckoo-land twaddle is a figure hard to contemplate. It is hardly harmful porn, and it is possible that its saccharine distortions of life as she is lived provide many with a welcome release from the mundane banality of their own lives. On the whole, however, chucking a Barbara Cartland seems a far less heinous literary offence than splitting an infinitive.

The *jeunesse dorée* of South Australia was, by all accounts, vastly amused, decided that libraries were not the stuffy, boring old places they had assumed them to be, and are now thronging them during the long hot summer holidays. They have, of course, realized subsequently that the book-chucking was a one-off exercise, and would be ill-advised to indulge in similar behaviour with an F. E. Edmonds opus.

It never rains but it pours. Not only was the cricket profoundly disappointing but then we heard that Britain's *White Crusader* had been knocked out of the elimination rounds for the America's Cup, and would therefore not be contesting the semi-finals. Far more of a shock to the world of twelve-metre racing was the elimination of the New York Yacht club's *America II* by young Kiwi genius Chris Dickson. Proving that Australian cricket captains are not the only breed of sportsmen liable to break down and sob, John Kolius, the NYYC skipper, could hardly conceal his emotion as he was obliged to concede defeat. After twenty-four successful defences of the Cup in the 132 years preceding *Australia II*'s 1983 victory in Newport, it seemed almost inconceivable that the NYYC should be eliminated from the competition at such an early stage. For five of the eight legs of the course, Kolius looked set to keep the glimmering hopes of reaching the semis burning, but in the end the vagaries of the sea breeze, the moody Fremantle Doctor, delivered the death blow. Twenty million dollars' expenditure and two years' preparation down the New York equivalent of the Swanee, their syndicate spokesman nevertheless managed an attempt at humour. The NYYC, he stated, was considering suing the Doctor for malpractice.

The Bond syndicate's executive director, Warren Jones, whose sense of history laudably outweighed any residual bitter memories he may have harboured of vicious squabbles with the NYYC over *Australia II*'s winged keel, went so far as to admit that he 'felt quite sad about it'. Not half as sad as John Kolius, clearly, but an admirable expression of sentiment all the same.

Less melancholic were two Sydney ex-pats now living in New York, who turned up at the 142-year-old NYYC in their cups to offer the establishment a replacement one. The Club declined their alternative trophy. It was a wooden spoon and Aussie flag sticking out of an empty can of Fosters.

On to Tasmania. From the air, it reminded me of the Highlands and Islands of Scotland. Tasmania was surrounded by mists and icy water, a verdant green island mounted like an emerald in uncompromising black onyx. The white-capped sea looked fierce as we circled over

Hobart, and thoughts turned to all those characters, a few sandwiches short of a picnic, who would set off on the Sydney/Hobart yacht race on Boxing Day whilst the rest of us were in bed nursing well-earned hangovers.

The Australians tell jokes about the Tasmanians the way the English tell jokes about the Irish, the French Belgians tell jokes about the Flemish Belgians, the Americans tell jokes about the Puerto Ricans, and everybody tells jokes about the Jews. The butts of the jibes are generally far brighter than the perpetrators, but there are nevertheless some good Tazzie tales worth repeating. For example, Tasmania is such a small and under-populated island that stories of inter-marriage, incest, cleft palates and clubbed feet are rife. Every Tasmanian is supposed to bear a scar, the resultant keloid tissue from the extra head the surgeons are obliged to remove at birth.

My favourite bad-taste story is the one about the young man who came home one evening and told his father that he was not going to marry the girl next door after all.

'And why not?' queried the father, a friend of the fiancée's family.

'She's a virgin,' answered the son.

'Then you are quite right,' said the father. 'If she's not good enough for them, she's not good enough for us.'

7

Canberra and Melbourne

Spirits were high to the point of giddiness as we reached the manufactured Australian capital of Canberra to play a one-day fixture against the Prime Minister's Invitation XI. A pillow fight erupted spontaneously on the bus and hitherto unspoken alliances demonstrated themselves more tangibly in the battle lines drawn. Beefy Botham at the back was immediately joined by Graham Dilley to launch a blistering attack on the front. There is, perhaps because of the blond wavy hair and the perennial sun specs, an uncanny clone resemblance developing between the two of them, and certainly Dilley seems smitten with no uncertain degree of hero-worship.

Canberra is one of those soulless cities specifically created as capitals to obviate the inter-state rivalries of more obvious candidates. Neither Melbourne nor Sydney would ever agree to the appointment of the other, and so an entirely new place had to be put on the map. Few people seem wont to spend much time there, and a cross-section of population would probably reveal an average of about ten civil servants to every normal citizen. For a swift visit, however, the tree-lined boulevards are far from ugly, and the many manifestations of civic pride are suitably impressive. The new Parliament building currently under construction is causing no small degree of resentment, however, as price estimates are gobbled up with the speed of comestibles anywhere within the physical proximity of Mike Gatting. An exorbitantly expensive new flagpole is also causing ructions, and it is interesting to see how bureaucrats living in ivory towers succumb to excess with the poor taxpayers' money.

Spirits were still high even as the manager organized a three-line whip to round up the team for a cocktail party at the Prime Minister's residence, The Lodge. It was, after all, only three days away from Christmas, and the festive spirit had already begun in earnest. The booze flowed freely, although reformed character, Bob Hawke, partook of none. A gifted cricketer himself, the Prime Minister takes great delight in spotting new talent, and his Invitation XI has been the launch pad for many young aspiring Australian hopefuls.

Of aspiring young Australian hopefuls there were indeed many, but not half as many as there were of press men, television men and camera crews trailing their coils of spaghetti wire behind them. Mr Hawke is certainly not unaware of the value of public relations, although whether constant hobnobbing with sportsmen of variegated degrees of brilliance is the right PR for a Head of State or Government is a moot point. Certainly I would not expect our own Leaderene, Mrs Thatcher, to know who every member of the England cricket team was, which is fair enough. It is debatable whether every member of the England cricket team would know who she was, either.

The cocktail nibbles were based on the Pritikin formula, a diet craze that has not yet hit the United Kingdom with quite the force it seems to have acquired here in Oz: 'Pritikin' baby pizzas, 'Pritikin' chicken balls and all the 'Pritikin' equivalents of the noxious junk we generally eat. The diet is simple enough: no fat, no salt and no sugar, and if Bob Hawke is anything to go by, it has a lot to recommend it. He is quite indisputably a charming man, not as tall as I had imagined, with thick, wavy, grey hair and rugged, lined features which speak volumes for his pre-

Pritikin days. A Rhodes Scholar who rose through the Australian Council of Trades Unions (ACTU) to leadership of the Australian Labor Party, he was on election in 1983 hailed as Australia's most popular politician ever. Three years in office have done plenty to put paid to such claims, and many people now feel he is losing the grass-roots support of the party. He has until 1988, however, to turn the tide of popularity in his favour once more, and sorting out the currently dicey Australian economy must remain his number one priority. A Treasurer who goes around shooting his mouth off about the country being on the brink of banana republicanism does not, unfortunately, tend to help Mr Hawke in this onerous endeavour.

There was much collegiate wincing in the ranks of the British High Commission contingent as Mike Gatting made his thank-you speech. Unlike the British press corps, they did not so much take exception to the many 'tremendouslies' and 'basicallies', but more to Gatt's constant and erroneous *lapsus linguae* in referring to the Prime Minister as the 'Premier'. It patently takes more than Rhodes Scholar Prime Ministers to impress our chaps, but the best was yet to come. Phillip DeFreitas, perhaps a trifle confused by the putting green the Hawkes had just installed at the bottom of the garden, rang home excitedly to relate that he had just had the privilege of meeting Bob Hope!

The next day, a capacity crowd of eight thousand packed the Makuna Oval for the most delightful day of cricket this tour. Police in tracksuits and Charlie Brown hats, the usual cricketer mufti, mingled discreetly with the crowd, as the Prime Minister sat quite relaxed outside the members' pavilion. It is difficult to think of too many countries in the world where this almost security-free movement is possible for a Head of Government.

A local radio station sponsor provided the sky-divers, who descended on the pitch to deliver the coin which the Prime Minister duly tossed before the start of play. Nubile young females in bikinis and shorts, sporting gaily coloured hats, sun visors and sun-deflecting umbrellas were much in evidence. It was a scorcher. Photographers wearing Foreign Legion caps complete with protective back flaps broiled lobster-red in the relentless sunshine. The pungent smell of meat barbecueing on the charcoal grills around the periphery of the ground hung heavily in the sultry atmosphere. Radio commentary references to the swimming-pool end came as welcome aural refreshment. The 'Jack Fingleton' scoreboard, the only comprehensible scoreboard I have seen in Australia, stood stark and massive in its black-and-white simplicity. Scoreboards at the Melbourne and the Sydney cricket grounds speak silent volumes of the thrusting technological developments that have so infiltrated the glorious summer game of late. As if the sight of Tony Greig and his Rexona Weather Wall (complete with temperature meter, humidity meter, wind direction meter, light meter and players' comfort meter . . . whatever that may mean) were not sufficient to strike apoplexy into the more conservative breasts of NW8, these monumental sports stadia now boast scoreboards with more dials than the Concorde and more lights than 'Sunday Night at the London Palladium'. There are instant replays, a source of often excruciating embarrassment to the often excruciating umpires. There are little yellow ducks that waddle on and off, blubbing, when a chap is out without making a score. There are advertisements for Diet Coke starring that most refreshingly extrovert of the Aussie cricketers, off-spinner Greg Matthews, and advertisements for the 'Clashes for the Ashes' starring 'my dear old thing' Henry 'Blowers' Blofeld, one of my favourite whimsical commentators. There is an instant statistical recall function, which will tell you everything bar a player's inside leg measurement, but is probably even programmed to do that as well if requested. Often the only thing that interrupts the entertainment is the cricket being played out in the middle.

Gaggles of children, more intent on collecting autographs than paying any attention to the game in progress, clustered around the players' enclosure.

'Mr DeFreitas!' shouted one precocious, if polite, ten-year-old with a spiky, lavatory-brush crew cut. 'Mr DeFreitas, please sign this for my autistic sister!'

'I'll set my wife on you,' threatened Philippe-Henri, suddenly tired of his quota of requests.

'You're Emburey, aren't you?' asked one real aficionado, incomprehensibly proffering Phil a copy of Allan Border's book for signature.

'Edmonds,' corrected Phil.

'Yes,' nodded the fan knowledgeably. 'John Edmonds'.

In deference to the fellow's patently encyclopaedic knowledge of the game and its exponents, Phil signed the book 'Don Bradman'.

Meanwhile I was busily interviewing the Prime Minister outside the members' pavilion. There is no doubt about it, he is a most approachable and personable politician. His current lifestyle, based on a strict regime – plenty of exercise, absolutely no booze and little sleep – has resulted in a certain Dorian-Gray-in-reverse effect: past pictures of him look fairly decadent, whilst the current model looks extremely good. He is generous in his praise of the administrative team which supports him, and reckons that one of the lessons he has learned over the years is the ability to delegate combined with the intuition to delegate to the right people.

'I've also learned how to catnap. During my time at the ACTU I often used to sleep through lunch, and even now I manage to catch the odd fifteen or twenty minutes' catnap.'

I could sympathize with him readily. Sleeping through trade union lunches seemed the only sensible way of dealing with them.

'What', I asked the Prime Minister, 'were the differences between Bob Hawke, most popular Australian politician ever in 1983, and Bob Hawke, 1987 vintage?'

'Well, I'm older,' he remarked wryly, a classic politician's statement of the obvious, 'and of course I am so much healthier than I was when I came to power.'

Mr Hawke has clearly learned, along with the Kissingers, and the Thatchers, that relentless stamina, possibly even more than genuine genius, is the quality which stamps most achievers, and certainly the majority of politicians who make it to the top.

'What we really have to get right', added the PM, 'is the economy. When we have sorted that problem out, there will be more money available for all these other policies . . . social and regional.'

That 'when', I suggested, might well be the operative word. A recent survey had shown that Australia, once the envy of the entire world, was now the largest debtor country on earth after Mexico and Brazil.

Such statistics seemed to have a dampening effect on the interview, so we watched the cricket for a while, and chatted amiably to the British High Commissioner, Sir John Leahy, the most affable of diplomats, and not the sort of chap you'd expect to thump photographers at Heathrow. I left the PM to enjoy the rest of David's innings in peace. It was, after all, Bob's day off, and we were, after all, playing Bob's own team, and no one, after all, would have asked Mrs Thatcher about Merseyside unemployment at her own son's wedding.

'Percy Fender' Gower, incidentally, won the Man of the Match award for that sparkling performance. It was, quite appropriately, a champagne bucket.

It was the day before Christmas Eve, and hot mince pies and Christmas cake were doing the rounds in the Ansett Golden Wings lounge as we waited for our flight to Melbourne. On this occasion, peace and good will to all men even extended as far as the press corps, and they too were allowed in to partake of the festal spirit.

We were staying once again in the Menzies at Rialto Hotel, where a disembodied synthetic voice in the lift, sounding disturbingly similar to Ted Heath at his most pompous, aggravatingly apprises you of every floor you reach. Surely the real Ted cannot have fallen so far out of favour as to be reduced to this? Voices in lifts, and omni-present muzak penetrating coffee shops, restaurants and even the deepest recesses of the bathroom seem to be a common feature of Australian, indeed nowadays of most international hotels. I find this constant noise nuisance perfectly infuriating, even tension-creating – surely the very opposite of the atmosphere it is designed to encourage.

It is quite possible, of course, that some people need constant external distraction. I was comparing notes with Lindsay Lamb the other day, and discovered that both Philippe-Henry and Lamby operate in the same way in the morning: that is, on the basis of maximum possible noise. Immediately on waking, they switch on both the television and the radio, just to ensure that neither is completely intelligible, and then, having woken up the sleeping partner with the resultant racket, they retire to the bathroom to read the paper in peace. Peace! There would be no need for peace if they had not unleashed the broadcasting babble in the first place.

Similarly, in transit more than half the team feel the need to keep the old Walkman plugged into the pinna, although the quality of conversation perpetrated by the other half proves this to be no bad idea. It often seems, however, that all this extraneous input is merely a substitute for any real cerebral activity. Myself, I have never been sucked into this Walkman craze. I far prefer to sit and think. Ideally, of course, I prefer just to sit.

Christmas Eve was spent putting the finishing touches to the costumes for the fancy-dress party. Such a degree of painstaking effort, of finely focused attention to detail, of well-rehearsed strategy and orchestrated design, has certainly never been a feature of England's preparations for a mere Test match.

We awoke on Christmas Day to open our presents. In the case of Les Edmonds this did not take long. Scrooge Edmonds had bought me nothing. Miraculously, all his credit cards expired two weeks after the inception of the tour, which is presumably why he wanted me along in the first place. Conscious of this parlous, state of pecuniary affairs, I had bought him nothing in return. I am not a woman to embarrass a man in penury.

Festivities kicked off at eleven o'clock with a pre-luncheon cocktail party given for the team by the press.

Cynics in the team wonder whether this is a tacit act of contrition (without any accompanying firm purpose of amendment) for all the times the press has stuffed them over the past twelve months. Cynics in the press wonder why they should be wasting their money on a bunch of people who would rather do anything than talk to them anyway. Three Buck's Fizzes apiece, however, and the twenty-four-hour yuletide bonhomie starts to flourish. 'The Street of Shame' moves swiftly into its production of 'A Christmas Carol', subtitled 'The Big Sleep' in honour of Mike Gatting's now celebrated lie-in during the State match against Victoria.

Dominic Allen, whose mellifluous tones will be familiar to listeners of LBC radio, is doing a splendidly stentorian job as narrator in setting the scene. There, in the middle of a Menzies at Rialto bedroom, stands a Menzies at Rialto look-alike bed, on which, covered completely by a large Menzies at Rialto duvet, lies an amorphous, heaving heap, which from time to time emits a loud, sonorous snore.

Littered around the bedroom are half a dozen breakfast trays piled high with, amongst other things, a couple of dozen bread rolls.

Buttons (presumably on loan from another pantomime, and anyway this has been written by the press, so who on earth expects the facts to be absolutely straight?) enters the bedroom carrying yet another breakfast tray. In a previous incarnation Buttons may well have been Graham Otway of *Today*.

Loud banging on the door and ringing at the bell ensues. Enter Burke and Hare, super-sleuths, looking for a titil-lating titbit, on this so far excruciatingly well-behaved tour.

Again, Burke and Hare bear more than a passing resem-blance to Paul Weaver of the *Mirror*, and Graham Morris, freelance sports photographer.

Frantic efforts are made to wake the captain, but to no avail. For it is time for Martin Johnson of the *Independent* to have his own words come back to haunt both him and the dormant England cricket captain.

The Three Ghosts of English Cricket appear in sequence. First, the Ghost of 'Can't Bat', played by Johnson himself. 'Can't Bat', says the Ghost to the snoring shapeless mound, 'I used to dog you in your early years.'

Then the second Ghost of 'Can't Bowl' appears, played by Peter Smith of the *Mail*, with his arm ostentatiously in a sling. He wants to know why Phil Edmonds never gets a bowl before tea. (Offstage, a raucous woman's voice is shouting, 'Phil, you boring old fart!' – 'It's the wicked witch of the press box,' they all chorus. 'She's been at the EEC wine lake again!')

Finally, trying unsuccessfully to upstage everyone else is Chris Lander of the *Sun*, usually Ian Botham's ghost, now appearing, by his kind permission, as the Ghost of 'Can't Field'.

'Do you have a sister?' asks another member of the cast. An embarrassed, hushed silence suddenly descends over the entire audience, as everyone waits to see how that will be received in the Botham camp. Ghosts of Miss ex-Barbadoses past still loom extremely large.

Next, there is a guest appearance by David Gower, doing a perfect take-off of himself clutching a bottle of Bollinger, tossing a coin, incomprehensibly murmuring 'Peter May says this. Peter May says that', and wandering on and off the set quite aimlessly lost. (Yet another ghost of West Indies past.)

Suddenly, Mike Gatting (portrayed by David Norrie of the *News of the World*, playwright extraordinaire, and impresario behind this entire production) awakens. His face is white with fear. The three Ghosts of England Cricket have shaken him badly. He is, nevertheless, still extremely well padded with help from a few extra pillows. Terror, in this instance, had involved no weight loss. He promises that, if the Ghosts will cease to haunt him, he will renounce all clichés during press conferences, and presumably all 'basicallies', 'tremendouslies', and 'lads-doing-good-jobs' as well.

It was good-humoured stuff, with that little didactic sting in the tail which relatively uncommunicative captains would ignore at their peril. Let us face it. Every pressman in the business needs his X hundred words by a deadline, and as the brighter Foreign Office spokesmen in delicate situations have learned, the more of those words you give to the majority of those as-lazy-as-the-rest-of-us journalists, the more chance *your* version of events has of percolating through.

Watered and humoured, members of the team then withdrew to change. Phil and I donned our jail-bird convict outfits, complete with ball and chain and manacles, and descended to the function-room. The entire Australian press and an avalanche of photographers was waiting for us all as we arrived. I told them we had come as Australians. When all is said and done, Aussies like to be reminded that they *do* have a cultural heritage.

People had gone to quite unconscionable lengths to come up with a winner. David Gower, Secretary of the Social Committee, looked disgracefully good as a Nazi SS officer, and demonstrated a masterful dominance and discipline in conducting proceedings which six months earlier would have kept him in the England captaincy job. Boyishly slim in black leather jackboots, tight-fitting jodhpurs, with unruly blond curls springing from underneath his uniform cap, he looked every inch the ascetic Aryan. An equivalent of 'Disgusted from Tunbridge Wells' wrote to the *Mail* deploring such an outfit, but coming from the reader of a paper whose views are not infrequently to the right of Sir Joh Bjelke-Petersen, we all found that quite amusing.

Vicki, David's fiancée, instantly converted to a nun, looked most fetching, though the fag hanging out of the side of her mouth was a bit of a giveaway.

Mike Gatting emerged with a flourish of silk and feathers as a Musketeer. 'All for one and one for all,' he shouted enthusiastically. It was abundantly clear that certain members of the England camp hadn't the foggiest what he was talking about.

Pushed along in wheelchair by Gatt was Graham Dilley, leaving a foaming trail of bubbly behind him. He had somehow managed to excavate large holes out of a rubbery white bathing cap, and had pulled it close on to his head so that his own thick blond hair only appeared in sporadic tufts. He was also linked up to an intravenous drip of Bollinger, presumably to cut out the middle-man. The press erroneously assumed Graham to be playing an intensive-care case, but far from being a common or garden patient, he was, in fact, impersonating our own dear Fender, whose golden locks are apparently going the way of PHE's.

Chris Broad looked tall and dignified as a splendid Wise Man, the role he has played all tour in his stalwart opening bat position. Bill Athey, serious and meticulous by nature, made an excellent school teacher, and Janet, his wife, charmingly cheeky in a *very* short gymslip, was billed as teacher's pet.

The Lambs' appearance as the Sugar Plum Fairies created a commotion. I had watched Lindsay, whose stores of patience and application seem boundless, as she stitched the costumes by hand one rainy afternoon in Tasmania. From two pink T-shirts, an infinity of tulle and a couple of cans of spray glitter, she had managed to create tutus that would not have disgraced Fonteyn in *Swan Lake*.

Lamby, on the other hand, who had refused to wear his co-ordinated pink tights, and was from time to time showing the odd flash of bare buttock juxtaposed with bright white jock strap and whatever it encompassed, was presumably playing a middle-order Nureyev in *The Nutcracker*.

Wilf Slack arrived as a sailor, but was shortly to be elevated to a more eminent position. Jack Richards looked fearsome as a Red Indian, and his wife Birjitta, disguised as Indiana Jones, the Raider of the Lost Ark, complete with Akubra hat and bull whip, was confusingly androgynous.

John Emburey looked suitably devious as Rasputin, and

Neil and Romany Foster came in dirty macs and plastic pigs' heads, carrying grubby cigarettes and filthy notepads and purporting to be the 'gutter press'.

Gladstone Small turned up as a very affluent-looking sheikh, with his Australian fiancée, Lois, as a very revealing member of his harem.

Bruce French, ever the merry man, took a leaf out of Sherwood Forest, and came as his county compatriot Robin Hood.

Lawrie Brown swashbuckled in as a very debonair Errol Flynn, Tasmania's favourite son and my posthumous hero after discovering one of his many villas had been named 'Cirrhosis by the Sea'.

Peter Lush, who had been landed with the difficult letter Q on which to base his costume, made an excellent QC. Certainly, he has a portly and dignified bearing, somewhat like Rumpole of the Bailey, which inspires great confidence. Mrs Lush came as the Queen of Hearts, and their daughter Amanda, who has been out here for the duration of the tour working for PBL marketing, came as a well-padded American football quarter back.

Septuagenarian scorer Peter Austin was a riot, in nothing but cardinal red underpants and an old blue mac, purporting to be a dirty-old-man-cum-flasher. His wife Gill, complete with apron and curlers, made a brilliant Coronation Street Hilda Ogden.

The Botham family, complete with three children and nanny, hopped along as the Bunbury Bunnies, inspired by actor David English's children's books of that name. All dressed in hand-made balaclavas and large, floppy ears, with blackened noses and whiskers stencilled on their faces, they made a charming picture. One-year-old Becky made not a sound as she munched her way through a quite considerable lunch for such a little tot. Paterfamilias Bunny Botham, magnificent furry extrusions sticking out of his head, and keeping the kids in check with the odd look, was quite a different animal in a domestic role few people ever witness.

By far the funniest entry, for my money, was Micky Stewart. Instantly christened as 'Sieg Heil' by the team for his rather less relaxed attitude to nets than that exhibited by last year's assistant manager, Bob Willis, Micky had elected to maintain the despotic image with a commendable shot at Julius Caesar.

It was unfortunate, however, that the theatrical costumiers of Melbourne demonstrated little in the way of classical education. It is doubtful whether any *civis romanus* worth his *sal*, let alone an *Imperator*, would have been caught dead in the baths wearing a synthetic, flaming carrot wig to support his laurels. Micky, whose imperial garb was every colour under the sun bar purple, looked hilarious, and a prime candidate for any *Carry on up the Forum* remake.

James Whitaker, in a thick black wig, a short black frock, fishnet tights and suspenders, made such a brilliantly tarty Lolita that there were suggestions of sending him to work the Cross when we got to Sydney. Poor James. He has had little enough opportunity to do much else of note this tour. Phil genuinely rates him as an excellent young batsman, but sadly his one opportunity to impress, during the third Test in Adelaide, did not come off. It would be comforting to think he might be given another chance next season.

The show-stealer, however, was without a shadow of a doubt Phillip DeFreitas, who minced in as a disturbingly epicene Diana Ross. In a curly black wig, a long, clinging, red satin evening dress, diamanté accessories, a feather boa, and make-up courtesy of Lois, there was only a moustache between him and a hell of a pile of trouble.

'How on earth do you girls walk around in things like these?' he asked, showing me a black, size 9 diamond-studded shoe, with a modest half-inch heel. A man more at home in a pair of Nikes, he looked truly horrified when I assured him that before certain very tall ladies married certain very gnome-sized heirs to the throne, we all used to teeter around in stilettos six times as high.

It was all back-slappingly merry as Gauleiter David, whose clipped Teutonic tones implied vays of making us enjoy ourselfs, yah!, distributed the Christmas presents. Wilf Slack was given an instant Archbishop Tutu outfit, comprising gold horn-rimmed spectacles and a dog collar. David awarded himself a tube of champagne toothpaste, and Lawrie received some of the rum-flavoured variety. Micky was given a can of disintegrating bullshit, certainly no reflection on his generally sagacious counsel, and Peter Austin snapped up his copy of *Wicked Willie's Guide to Women* with obvious fervour. Gladstone, who apparently cannot swim, was given a pair of water-wings and the manager was presented with a beer-gut ruler. Gatt, inevitably, was quite overburdened with diet books, copies of the *Australian Gourmet* magazine if these failed, and a special alarm clock in the form of a candle, the operating instructions of which would be better left to the reader's imagination.

Bill Athey was awarded a rubber brick, on which, in the future, he could vent his frustrations. Chris Broad got a book on the natural superiority of the left-hander, and Graham Dilley, a heavy smoker, received a cigarette in a case bearing the legend 'in an emergency, break glass'. Mr and Mrs Manager were apparently thrilled with their His and Hers mugs. Bruce French, who apart from hardly playing a game this trip, has also had the misfortune of ending up in a Tasmanian hospital with an acute chest infection, accepted a copy of *How to Survive in Australia* with cheery stoicism.

The Fosters eyed their 'Fundies' with some alarm – an intimate piece of underwear with holes to accommodate four legs at once. Phil accepted the various tomes on terminal hair loss with relatively good grace, as indeed he did the game 'How to Become a Billionaire'. (Answer included inside: a screw, and underneath the word 'everybody'.)

Ian Botham, unaccountably, was presented with a game entitled 'Grass', and his wife Kathy, who had recently appeared modelling in the *Sun*, was presented with a pneumatic set of Samantha Foxesque boobs.

Gradually, the humour began to degenerate along somewhat more lavatorial lines. There was plenty of farting-foam knocking around, not to mention various pairs of edible knickers (piña colada, rum and banana flavoured). A pet cock was also presented, together with a copy of *100 Games to Play with your Pussy*. For the well-endowed (I am obliged to accept this on hearsay) there were elephant-trunk undies, and for the once-endowed but clearly no longer so, there was a patented virginity restorer, together with the message 'Crude, horny, tramp! When will I see you again?'

To general acclaim, Peter Austin was granted a *summa cum laude* 'Dirty Old Man's Certificate', and little black books and large black condoms were also distributed. It was then that some idiot gave Both a can of bright green hair spray . . .

Meanwhile the Australian team was, presumably, enjoying a traditional Christmas smoulderingly resenting the in-laws, and silently wanting to strangle the kids.

The next day, Boxing Day, the remarkably successful Dilley was unfit to play in this, the fourth Test, and was replaced by Gladstone Small, who amply rewarded selectorial confidence with a haul of five wickets in the Australians' first innings, and was to end up with the Man of the Match award. The Australian selectors came in for the expected criticism, and were generally berated for playing batsmen who could bowl a bit, and bowlers who could bat a bit, and generally fielding a side, as Mike Gatting aptly described it, of bits and pieces players. Those who had not already fallen to bits looked likely soon to fall into pieces. Certainly, none of the England team could understand quite why the best Aussie middle-order batsman, Greg Ritchie, was omitted, only to be recalled as an opener for the next test in Sydney. It was in all the same sort of incomprehensibly erratic selection policy which had so hallmarked England's jittery selectors in the West Indies and, in the following season, against India and New Zealand. It is the hokey-cokey school of selection; put a man in, take a man out, and generally just shake 'em all about, an empirical approach to a problem rather than a concentrated effort to solve it.

Suffice it to say, England won the match in two-and-a-half days, thus taking an invincible two-nil lead in a best-of-five series, and retaining the Ashes.

Most players had long since returned to the hotel from the booze-sodden dressing-room by the time Phil tipped up, a good five hours after stumps were drawn. By about nine o'clock, tired of waiting for the conquering hero to return, I went downstairs to hail a taxi and go to Chinatown for dinner with Peter Roebuck and Matthew Engel. Suddenly a car screeched to a halt, Fittipaldi-style, outside the hotel, and who should emerge but Both, Both's dad, Both's agent, Elton John (looking impeccable in a light grey, double-breasted silk suit, which had somehow managed to absorb a magnum or two of dressing-room champagne projectiles and still look good) and Philippe-Henri.

It was perhaps fourteen years since I had last seen Phil well and truly plastered. On that occasion, an all-male Cambridge University dining club, 'The Drones' (a wonderfully suitable title, reflecting on the members), had been busily giving it some hammer at the Pink Geranium. Phil is a large man, so large that if it should one day occur to him, similarly smashed, to wander round Epping Forest, people would probably queue up to claim sightings of the Missing Link. In physique, to put it bluntly, he is in the Neanderthal mould, which coincides with the majority of his attitudes.

In those days, however, I used to be quite glad to see the old boy, though on one occasion not sufficiently be-rosy spectacled as to welcome the sight of him creating uproar at four in the morning, very much under the influence, and in an all-women's college from which men were officially disgorged by midnight.

He had hopped over a few walls, and side-stepped a few porters and come to wish me good night. You better believe it! By this stage he was incapable of doing much else. I was awakened by the splintering sound of a door being cloven in two, as Edmonds tapped for admission.

It was difficult to know what to do with fifteen stone of inebriated, if not unaffectionate, stupor. Any attempt to get him out past the porters again was to risk certain discovery. Besides, there was no way he could be let loose on the Huntingdon Road and the good townies of Cambridge. To allow him to stay, on the other hand, was to court an entire women's college's nocturnal disruption. *En suite* bathrooms are not a feature of undergraduates' rooms, and New Hall was quite obviously about to witness, albeit in regurgitated form, an entire Pink Geranium à la carte menu.

The decision was summarily taken out of my hands, as PHE, making valiant if redundant effort to remember some of the no doubt sparkling conversation to which he had been party that evening, opened the window, and decided on an exquisitely executed expectoration on to one of the college's prize herbaceous borders.

New Hall is a modern college, in the Frank Lloyd Wright mould, and the unmistakable sounds of much macho retching echoed hollowly around the white concrete dining-room dome, the magnificent goldfish ponds, the extensive waterways and the long, open corridors.

Matters were in no way helped by the fact that my tutor lived immediately above me. The tutor to which a Cambridge undergrad is assigned is generally of a totally different discipline from the one which the student is supposed to be pursuing. A Director of Studies directs academic performance, whilst a tutor is, putatively at least, *in loco parentis*, in charge of one's moral welfare.

My heart sank as I heard the window upstairs being hurriedly opened. A light spilt into the external darkness. Edmonds, never a brilliant conversationalist until he met Mike Brearley, and in those days about as garrulous as a giant clam, suddenly would just not shut up. By now he was proclaiming a future of undying love and affection, joint mortgages, and shared American Express bills, and equal partnership in anything I might earn. I was keenly aware of some lady academic's head projecting out of the window a mere one floor up, curlers poking out at all angles like so many tracking sensors, trying hard to ascertain the source of the demented warbling.

Eventually she pulled her head in. Phil immediately stuck his out. Aware of the continuing racket, she stuck hers out again. By this time seeing nothing, she pulled hers in again. By this stage we were at the crème caramel, coffee, liqueurs and after-eight-wafer-thin-mints course of the disgorged menu. He stuck his head out again. Terrified though I was of imminent rustication, I could not help but see the funny side of it. The pair of them reminded me of that Swiss invention, where a little man with a feather hat and a little woman in a dirndl skirt swivel in and out of an Alpine chalet to indicate the weather forecast.

Now, fourteen years later, old Edmonds was doing a repeat performance. Wearing no shoes, ex-ophthalmic eyes revolving in opposite directions, he was hallucinating badly, and claiming sightings of P. B. H. May, who as far as anybody knew was no longer with us, though admittedly it is difficult to tell.

'We've won the Ashes. We've won the Ashes!' he proclaimed loudly to the entire lobby.

I was for once the only person around to be dead cold-stone sober, and extremely peeved to be so.

'You've *retained* the Ashes,' I corrected, prissily pedantic. It is easy to play semantics when you're sober.

'Yes, yes,' rejoined Phil, breathlessly excited. 'This is the happiest day of my cricketing life. Yes, this is the happiest cricketing of my daily life. Yes, this is the happiest living of my cricketing day . . .'

I thought by then we had heard most of the possible permutations of the Edmonds' exuberance, and decided to drag him off to bed before he could accost a vaguely alarmed Doug Insole with the Union Jack he had just acquired from some hanger-on.

Bravely carrying Phil's cricket coffin was Elton John. Accustomed to travelling with an entourage of minders, publicity agents, chauffeurs, valets, dressers and, on occasion, the entire Melbourne Symphony Orchestra, Elton had carefully packed Phil's kit himself, with a degree of neatness rarely seen in the P. H. E. wardrobe. As a gesture of gratitude, Phil in return had given Elton his cricket bat, which was in fairly pristine condition, at least around the middle.

From an Australian point of view, the fourth Test was, of course, a complete fiasco. After the usual drubbing of the selectors, the critics turned inevitably to the Australian captain Allan Border, or AB as he is generally known, and started calling for his blood. It was a classic case of *déjà vu*, reminiscent of the treatment meted out to his great friend, David Gower, while still captain of England last year. The analogy went still further. Both men, whilst copping the flak for just about everybody else's failures, were performing well themselves. Although Border has not, by his own astounding standards, had a brilliant series thus far, there is nevertheless plenty of statistical evidence to support the argument that he is one of the best players in Australian cricketing history. In the past eighteen months, for example, since the start of the 1985 tour of England, Border has scored twenty-three first-class centuries, nine coming in Tests. During the fourth Test at the MCG, he managed to reach a thousand Test runs in 1986, following the 1,099 he notched up in the previous calendar year. The Melbourne Test also witnessed Border's three thousandth run scored in first-class matches in 1986. Considering that he is one of the few Aussies with a definite place in the team, it is difficult to ascertain quite whom the bandwagon critics would have replace him.

We left everyone else to continue the party in Both's suite, and went to our room on the tenth floor, Phil, confused, talking to the voice in the lift and ordering its invisible owner to come out of hiding and show himself.

I must say, he is so much more amenable and affable a character when he has had a few that I do wish he would do it more often. He kept reciting a little ditty to himself, a limerick I had composed to the Australian wicketkeeper, Tim Zoehrer. To say Zoehrer had had a bad game would be charitable. It had been appalling. Tim also has a reputation on the circuit for giving it quite a touch of the verbals, or sledging, as it is more often called. At one stage during the match, while Phil was batting, he was hit on the pad, and the ball carried to silly mid-off. Zoehrer and a few of the slip-fielders went into a loud and somewhat exaggerated chorus of appeal. 'Don't be silly,' said Phil, to no one in particular, a broad smile expanding cheekily over his face. He had been adjudged out in Adelaide from exactly the same shot. 'You're not going to cheat me out again this time, are you?'

Young Zoehrer apparently went berserk. Mark Austin (ex-BBC newsman and now with ITN), who was listening to the entire scene from the Channel 9 control box, said he had never heard anything quite like it in his life. Phil, who is old enough to have played cricket with the likes of Thommo, Lillee, Marsh and the Chappells in their prime, had never heard anything quite like it either. Channel 9 has a microphone stategically planted right next to the wicket, so that TV viewers can hear the sweet sound of leather on willow, or the clickety-clunk of bails being removed. Fortunately, since few modern cricketers are wont to say 'Oh, dear me! What a silly shot!', or alternatively 'Goodness! I should not have thought that was really out!', there is a time-lag button placed on the device so that the only commentary viewers ever receive is that of former cricketers in the commentary box, rather than any gloss from current cricketers on the square. According to David Gower, however, the watchdog of the button only pays attention to the proceedings *during* overs. If you really want to screw the system and scandalize the far-more-shockable-than-we-are Aussies, all you have to do is go up to the wicket *in between* overs, and whisper, 'BUGGER, BUGGER, BUGGER'.

Be that as it may, Zoehrer's blue invective continued for the duration of Phil's innings, and was further exacerbated by Phil's asking Allan Border exactly who this young pup thought he was, why on earth he should have been picked in the first place, and why he did not concentrate his efforts on keeping wicket.

Poor Zoehrer. He was having a nightmare and no doubt feeling the pressure. Bay 13, the MCG equivalent of Manchester United's Stretford End, was heartlessly giving him a very hard time. If you think Australians enjoy a go at us Pommies from time to time, you should hear them slagging off one another. Inter-State rivalries and jealousies run very deep, and Tim, as a Western Australian, was getting very short shrift from a predominantly Victorian crowd barracking for its own man, Dimattina. Some critics went so far as to suggest that they would rather see *anyone* else, even the New South Welshman, Dyer, behind the stumps, which for Victorians was saying something.

When Phil returned that evening and recounted the episode to me, I thought it was amusing enough to deserve a few limericks, and accordingly penned the following:

> There was a young glove-man named Zoehrer,
> Whose keeping got poorer and poorer,
> Said AB from first slip,
> 'Please stop giving such lip,
> And with extras stop troubling the scorer!'

With a glorious indifference to even the most elementary rules of scansion, the England dressing-room got hold of this, and rearranged the last line to embrace as many 'fucks' as possible.

The second limerick, which had my preference, found less favour:

> Bay 13, they shout 'Dimattina,
> This Zoehrer keeps like a cretina,
> And we'd rather they choir,
> 'Have that other clown, Dyer,
> Than Zoehrer, who is a has-beener'.

In any event, Phil, after consultation with the England middle-order Muses, took the verses into the Australian dressing-room and read them both out. It occasioned, apparently, some degree of mirth. The Australian team, don't forget, are not all Western Australians, either.

To Zoehrer's credit, he responded in kind, and by lunch-time had composed his own riposte:

> There was a balding old man called Philippe,
> Who stands in the gully too deep,
> When his turn came to bat
> He opened his trap,
> And his innings just fell in a heap.

It was unfortunate that a couple of Australian papers got hold of this exchange of literature, and turned the good-humoured mickey-taking into an Edmonds/Zoehrer hate campaign. Some of the papers concerned went even so far as to give to Botham, of all people, the paternity of the original limericks. Not for the first time I was encouraged to dwell on the dislocation between the facts and what people read in the newspapers. And not for the last time were my poetic efforts to occasion a few sparks.

8

Perth: the Benson and Hedges Challenge

Inured, as the England team was in the West Indies series, to two-and-a-half-day Test matches, the truncated Melbourne game came as a particularly welcome respite to them in this dizzy Australian itinerary. Two genuine free days. No nets. No hiding from the press in the bar. The sweet and unaccustomed taste of success at last.

Two days later, however, we were on the transcontinental move again, back to Perth for the Benson and Hedges so-called 'Spinnaker' Challenge.

Manager Peter Lush was his jovial self as usual, but nevertheless admitting to no mean degree of disappointment over an inexplicable silence from the corridors of power in London. If Bob Hawke had been the present incumbent of Number 10, all members of the victorious England team would no doubt have been awarded grace and favour homes by now, and Mike Gatting would doubtless have been elevated to the peerage: Lord Gatting of Branston (with due deference to his proclivities in pickle), would have made a very suitable title. As it was, the boys were surprised that they had failed to receive either a telex or a telegram of congratulations from either the British Prime Minister, Margaret Thatcher, or the Sports Minister, Richard

Tracey. I mentioned this in my *Times* diary, a full fortnight later, just to make sure that the Sir Humphrey Applebys of life had had a fair span to do the necessary.

About a month later (presumably after the offending article had been spotted in Cheltenham as subversive), Peter was duly informed that the Sports Minister had indeed despatched a telex, but it had apparently missed us. It is, of course, not very difficult to miss the England cricket team. They are an eminently missable group of sixteen players, three management, 135 pieces of luggage weighing over three and a half thousand pounds, six crates of wine, three crates of Johnnie Walker whisky, two crates of Hine cognac, a crate of 'Fender's Fizz', a large Liberty's hat box (mine), thirty items of hand luggage, a dozen wives and consorts, and about forty accompanying press and media folk. We slip in and out of airports and hotels with all the unobtrusive discretion of a Shirley Bassey frock. Anyway, miss us that telex certainly did!

Perth is fast becoming a second home to us, so often have we been here. As we flew in around 10 p.m. local time, we could see the illuminated WACA, where the Pakistanis were playing the West Indians in a day/night game, shining like a molten pool of platinum in the surrounding darkness.

The Sheraton-Perth lobby was in a mild state of bedlam. Accommodating one cricket team is bad enough, but accommodating four of them, plus the entire Channel 9 contingent, is stretching any hotel's reserves of goodwill to the limit.

Our corridor was a true league of nations: some members of the England team; some of the West Indian team; the ebullient Pakistani team; and, stuck unaccountably in the midst of us all, a newly-wed Japanese couple on honeymoon. It would be distressing to think that they left Australia with the impression that this set-up was a fair reflection of Western mores.

There is no point in pretending that these one-day games are anything other than a complete lottery. Bill 'Tiger'

O'Reilly, the great Australian leg-spinner and googly purveyor and the only Aussie to have played in all matches of the controversial Bodyline series, constantly dismisses these limited-over knockabouts as 'The Pyjama Game'. He is a grand old man, Tiger, and I had the pleasure of a long chat to him over dinner last time we were here. He is a delightful mixture of the conservative and the controversial, with that anti-establishment penchant so many of us second- or third-generation Irish seem to harbour. In his eighties he still stands very tall and erect, retains that certain Gaelic twinkle in the eye and readiness with the tongue which delights many and infuriates a few, and continues to write an extremely hard-hitting regular column for the *Sydney Morning Herald*.

The Pyjama Game is not an inaccurate visual assessment of the one-day international, Aussie style. Purists of the game still gag visibly at the sight of the gaily striped garb in which the teams are obliged to perform. England, in truth, do not look so bad. Their kit is predominantly light blue, sporting discreet yet distinctive dark-blue stripes. The trousers have never seen a natural fibre in their lives, and at thirty degrees centigrade in the shade must surely be responsible for many an adult version of nappy rash and galloping jock rot. Only men could dream up the idea of wearing synthetic fibres in these kinds of temperatures.

The Aussies must surely feel themselves at a distinct psychological disadvantage as they march on to the pitch trying to feel aggressive and on the contrary looking distinctly emasculated, swathed as they are in canary-yellow with a green stripe. Bearing a marked resemblance to a clump of etiolated daffodils does little to reinforce the much-sought macho Oz-sportsman image.

The Pakistanis, a very young side, look like the enthusiastic products of an expensive prep school in their bright green outfits slashed by counter-distinct blue stripes.

Maroon with grey, on the other hand, would have to be the last colours on earth any thoughtful couturier would slap together, but this is the dreadfully dull combination in which the West Indians appear. In normal circumstances the brightness of their cricket would outshine the drabness of their gear, but then this occasion was far from normal.

On New Year's Eve, the England team was obliged to practise in the afternoon, prior to their first match against Australia the following day. That evening, Elton John was throwing a party for us at the house of Lancashire and ex-England cricketer Graeme Fowler. 'Foxy', who seems, in cricketing terms at least, to have sunk without trace since a magnificent double century in Madras during England's triumphant 1984/5 tour of India, is currently working in a PR capacity here in Perth.

It was not entirely felicitous, therefore, that my publisher, Derek Wyatt, should have dropped in around about fourish for a cup of tea. Derek was out here from London for various reasons. First, he wanted to sign up Harold Cudmore for a book on twelve-metre racing; second, he wanted to ascertain what his two protégés, Le Roebuck and La Edmonds, were up to; third, he wanted to see Vic Marks (Somerset and England), at present doing extremely well for Western Australia; fourth, he wanted to catch up with Engel; fifth, he wanted to see some cricket; and sixth, it was minus ten degrees Fahrenheit in London.

'I'd like a cup of tea,' said Derek.

'I'd like a cup of tea, too,' said I.

'Waiter,' we chorused as one, 'bring us a bottle of something bubbly.'

It was a classic case of history repeating itself. Last year in the West Indies I should have learned the folly of trying to match an ex-England rugby international drink for drink . . .

I am given to believe that Elton's party was superb, with magnificent food and drink supplied by the Orchard Hotel. I cannot remember too much about it, however, except being rock 'n' rolled into the disco, and creating no small amount of fairly irreparable damage. Some time late the next morning, the list of New Year's resolutions started off in the time-honoured way . . .

The Australians played quite horribly, and were duly rewarded with the wooden spoon of the competition. The man on whom the fickle Australian supporters' opprobrium was most focused was the luckless Tasmanian opener, David Boon. In the match against the West Indies, for instance, this out-of-form batsman was hooted and jeered as he walked on to the pitch, not perhaps the sort of reception ideally designed to encourage a man to lift his game to new heights. Near the scoreboard, the wit and repartee flowed with the beer, as Boon managed to get off the mark with the first ball of the innings. 'You're seeing it like a watermelon, Boonie,' shouted one sarcastic fan. 'See the over out, David!' encouraged another.

It seemed like eternities later when the poor fellow, with a mere two to his name on the scoreboard, had his middle stump removed by a dazzler from Joel Garner. This precipitated even more flak form the WACA crowd. 'No wonder Tasmania is not a part of Australia,' harried the ultimate wag as Boon walked disconsolately back to the dressing-room. Inter-State knocking is indeed as cruel as anything the Aussies mete out to us.

The Aussie opening combinations were so consistently bad that David Gower's fiancée, Vicki, came up with the definition of an optimist: an Australian opening batsman who bothers to put zinc cream on his nose.

Neither was their bowling particularly penetrative, and the one enduring highlight of the entire challenge was the sight of Ian Botham laying into the new, young Victorian medium paceman, Simon Davis, knocking twenty-four off one over, and Davis off the selectors' short-list for a while to come.

With few exceptions, however, this superabundance of one-day internationals means that they all have a tendency to merge indistinguishably into one another. Even Henry Blofeld freely admits: 'We can all remember what happened in the Test matches, but, my dear old thing, who on earth can remember what went on in all those one-dayers?'

What we can, of course, remember is that England beat

the Australians, the West Indies (oh, sweet revenge) and the Pakistanis, to win the series. That was all very well and good, but did it really *mean* anything? For a start, the boisterously youthful Pakistanis, on a one-week release from the savage strictures of Islam Fundamentalism and the ever-watchful eye of the President, General Zia-ul-Haq, were busily giving it their very best shot until all hours in the Sheraton disco. The chances are that they could well prove an entirely different proposition in the full-blown Test series against England in the summer of 1987.

More significant still in putting the English victory in a less-hyperbolic-than-the-British-tabloids context, was the veto placed on bowling bouncers. The West Indians, in particular, were psychologically stumped by this blanket prohibition, and their team without that relentless mean-machine quartet of pace bowlers was certainly not the same animal which had so badly mauled us in the Caribbean on the last tour: Samson without the hair. The banning of all those intimidatory Exocets constantly whistling around the batsman's head had a salutary effect on the English line-up, but it was simultaneously instrumental in frustrating and depressing the Windies' fast bowlers. Negative sentiments (as England themselves saw in the Caribbean) have a distressing tendency to permeate an entire side, and the West Indian batsmen, who were already out of touch, were in turn affected. Once again, however, whilst the West Indies may not appear to be quite the force they were, particularly in the absence of Clive Lloyd, cricketers everywhere would be foolish to assume that an unbridled West Indian team would necessarily be the same toothless opponents in Test matches.

The Pakistani captain, Imran Khan, was inconsolable at his team's final loss to England, although admittedly it must be difficult for anyone to drown his sorrows in orange juice. At thirty-four, I have seen him quoted in various women's magazines (which of course I never purchase, but only ever read at friends' houses or in the dentist's) as one of the most eligible bachelors in the world. Certainly, women's magazines' goo apart, he would have to rate as the most eligible bachelor in the cricketing world, where the competition is somewhat more restricted. Oxford-educated, affluent, with those chiselled good looks of the Pakistani warrior caste, he was constantly inundated with female autograph-or-whatever-else-might-be-available hunters as he sat having a depressed chat with Phil and me. Actually, he was not so much surprised at the result. Last year, a palmist had foretold his future, and this was all part of it. No, his depression was far more deeply rooted than that. He had just suffered the break-up of a long-standing relationship with an English girl who eventually discovered that she could not embrace the Pakistani way of life, and Imran, arguably *the* most eligible bachelor in the world, had decided that he was now irretrievably on the shelf.

'And what is worse,' he confided morosely, 'is that I am even too old for an arranged marriage now. All the best ones have gone.'

We told Imran not to despair, and bought him another orange juice. Somehow it was difficult to avoid the feeling that he would finally make out.

Along the coast in Fremantle there was no shortage of gloom, doom and despondency, either. Just about everybody was worried about the apparently unbeatable form of the New Zealanders' fibreglass yachts, not least the mammoth fleet of American TV people who were petrified at the prospect of an Australian-Kiwi final. If the Kiwis were to beat Dennis Conner's *Stars and Stripes* for the right to challenge for the America's Cup, Stateside networks stood to lose up to U.S. $150,000,000 in advertising revenues and telecast outlays.

Quite a deal of anti-Kiwi feeling was being generated by the Australians themselves, and at least one of the syndicates was making no secret of the fact that they would rather lose the Cup to Big Bad Dennis and the San Diego Yacht Club than see it carried off to Auckland.

Maybe Conner himself, who has openly questioned the legitimacy of the fibre-glass hulls, started the ball rolling in earnest. Last week he was heard to dismiss a tenacious reporter, offhandedly: 'I've already said "no comment". What are you – stupid? Or are you just from New Zealand?'

The shopkeepers, hoteliers and restaurateurs of Freo are all in agreement, however. From a financial and tourist point of view, the final has to be between one of the Australian syndicates and the Americans' *Stars and Stripes*.

Depression, however, as you may readily imagine, was not the abiding characteristic of the England squad, as they boarded yet another plane for yet another transcontinental flight the morning after the final.

9

The Great Australian Ginger-Nut débâcle

Spirits were still buoyant as we reached the Sebel Town House in Sydney. Beating the Australians has become a commonplace event, but beating the Pakistanis, and *a fortiori*, beating our erstwhile drubbers, the mighty West Indians, albeit in a one-day lottery, was balm to last year's wounded team soul.

Released from hospital after throat surgery, and awaiting our arrival at the hotel, was Elton John. His childlike and unsophisticated pleasure at being with the cricketers is both touching and endearing, and he appears to enjoy the camaraderie of this extended family. I wonder, sometimes, whether despite his being surrounded by the usual superstar's coterie, the life of the successful pop idol is not an extremely lonely one. Much press speculation is being expended on the reasons why his wife Renata left Australia halfway through his tour, and on why she was not in attendance by his sick bed in his hour of need. We leave such society gossip to the relevant columnists. All we know is that Elton loves us, and we all love him.

He was waiting for us in the lobby, barred by his ENT consultant from talking for ten days after having nodules removed form his vocal cords. Wearing one of his large collection of wacky hats (this one sort of fez-shaped in ersatz zebra skin), he was hopping Ariel-like through the reception area, holding a placard on which he had carefully inscribed the words 'Great Result'.

It is an interesting mutual admiration society, that of Elton and the team. He likes being around in their company and they like being around in his: symbiotic groupies, really.

The Sebel Town House is not your common or garden cricket tour hotel. In no way ostentatious, small, understated and discreet, it is nevertheless the favourite watering-hole of many showbiz personalities, whose autographed photographs adorn the small and even excessively cosy bar. Megastars Dire Straits had even left a golden disc, which now adorns the lobby, in gratitude for the gracious hospitality and 'nothing-too-much-trouble' service they had received there. Certainly the Sebel was a welcome change from all those vast and impersonal establishments we have been wont to rest our weary cricket coffins in. It put me in mind of my favourite London hotel, the Berkeley, in Knightsbridge, where, swimming around in the rooftop pool one day, I spied a rather corpulent Henry Kissinger heaving, anonymously, in the one direction, and a recently married, unremarkable Dustin Hoffman racing in the other.

Sydney! This has got to be the most exhilarating city in Australia: the palpable buzz of business and commerce, the cosmopolitan zest of the place. Looking out over the harbour at the bridge and the Opera House, watching the myriad hordes of laser-boats, yachts, cruisers, ferries and hydrofoils, and hearing weather reports of Big Ben freezing up in London, it is not difficult to think in terms of emigrating.

The Australian selectors, now under quite intolerable pressure to produce a winning team overnight, have named a hitherto unknown New South Wales off-spinner, a certain P. Taylor, for the fifth and final Test, in ever more desperate efforts to salvage some pride out of the series. 'Peter who?' the headlines read the next morning. Suggestion abounded that the selectors had patently given up all hope of winning, decided to cut their losses, and to save on air fares by selecting any local lad. The British press had a field day, implying that the selectors had probably been at the Australian equivalent of the pink gin, and had made a mistake by naming the wrong Taylor, Peter instead of Mark. In the press box people wondered out loud whether they had not gone for A. J. P. Taylor, although not all were sure whether this eminent historian was still alive. Aberrant though Australian selectorial policy had clearly become, selection from the land of the living was still thought to be the bottom line.

Former Test great, Neil Harvey, had already started calling for the removal of 'unqualified' selectors from the panel a few weeks prior. He claimed that none of them, with the exception of Greg Chappell, had been through the mill as cricketers. 'Jim Higgs went through a tour of England without scoring a run,' he claimed in a newspaper interview. 'How on earth could he be a good judge of a batsman? Dick Guy played only a handful of games as a leg-spinner for NSW, and I remember Lawrie Sawle as a batsman for Western Australia who struggled to hit the ball back past the bowler.'

Harsh stuff indeed, although one assumes that a man who has himself served time as a selector, between 1967 and 1978, must know more or less what he is talking about.

The Test match, however, was going to be the least of my worries that week, for this was the week I was to co-host Channel 10's *Good Morning, Australia* breakfast television show with resident anchor man Gordon Elliot, as the regular hostess, Kerri-Anne Kennerley, was away on holiday in Europe. The whole idea had originally seemed like quite a wheeze.

Doing breakfast TV is a killer. I had never done anything like this before in my life, and in retrospect should have insisted on a minimum of a couple of hours' training before going national. After a week's experience I am sure that looking at camera X, reading autocue Y and doing interview

Z becomes a piece of cake. At any rate it cannot be more difficult than trying to unravel the linguistic macramé of a President Mitterrand when he is trying to obfuscate the sort of hoop through which we conference interpreters are regularly obliged to jump.

The first problem to contend with is getting up in the morning at about 4.30 a.m. Bad enough though this may be when living in a normal household configuration, with an upstairs, a downstairs, rooms to eat in, rooms to work in, and rooms to watch the television in, it becomes virtually impossible if you happen to be sharing a hotel bedroom with the most selfish man in the world. The Sebel was full, thanks to the Elton John travelling circus, and the Lionel 'dancing on the ceiling' Richie entourage, otherwise I should most certainly have moved into another room to get some sleep at night. As it was, Phil insisted on watching those educationally sub-normal productions they broadcast until midnight here on hotel television, and then reading until about 3 a.m. for good measure. When I left at 4.30 a.m., heady with lack of sleep, I would tiptoe around in the dark, clothes all neatly laid out beforehand, lest I should wake him. And to cap it all, Phil, who normally watches breakfast TV from its inception at 7 a.m., never bothered to watch it even once that entire week. Do you wonder I laugh when I hear accusations of failing to be a supportive wife? The only thing that ten years of marriage has taught me is that all this being supportive nonsense works in one direction only.

Gordon Elliot is a very large, very gifted, very talented man with a commensurately large ego. I like him a lot. It is rare to find genuinely funny people. He has hosted the show for almost six years now, and is moving on in two weeks' time to greater, more glorious things than breakfast TV. Anyone's private and social life must be seriously curtailed when a 4.30 a.m. morning start is mandatory, and he openly admits that he is leaving with few regrets.

The first morning we chatted about the larceny perpetrated in England's dressing-room at the Sydney

Cricket Ground, where, amongst other things, Ian Botham's custom-built three-pound bats had been liberated. Fortunately, batmaker and Worcestershire County Cricket Club committee member, Duncan Fearnley, was on hand, both to organize Botham's new county contract, and to replenish the lacunae in the bat situation.

'It's a special bat, with a three-black-condom-grip handle,' Duncan explained to me one evening. I repeated this knowledgeably to Gordon the next morning.

'The sort teams use in Barbados, I assume,' he rejoined, blue eyes twinkling behind steel-framed spectacles. He never missed a trick.

I have never fully understood who watches breakfast television. Certainly I only ever watch it when closeted in an hotel room, where the range of the radio is restricted to some dreadful demi-classical muzak and the inanities of the local radio station. Surely if people are on their way to work, they do not have time to sit and watch the box? And if they are not on their way to work, why bother to get up at 7 a.m. to watch two hours of trivial tales and enforcedly jovial chat? I, of course, am perfectly at liberty to think what I like. The statistics show that an estimated five million people get up every morning, switch on the telly, and watch *Good Morning, Australia*. In a country as sparsely populated as Australia, that is one helluva lot of people.

Dear Matthew Engel rang up surreptitiously to say 'well done' after the first programme. I say surreptitiously, because the received wisdom is that no cricket correspondent worth his media medal should see the light of day before 10 a.m. When England captain Mike Gatting overslept for the State game against Victoria the tabloid furore knew no bounds, but there were in fact no more than half a dozen journalists in the press box who had actually arrived at the ground in time to eyewitness his non-arrival. The degree of outrage expressed, however, was in general terms inversely proportional to the track record of punctuality demonstrated by any named correspondent. Oh, what a comatosely unsensational tour this has been! Last year in the West Indies, the press seemed almost pleasantly surprised when eleven Englishmen bothered to pitch up for the Test matches, let alone other matches, and the attendance level at 'optional nets' became synonymous with absolute *laissez faire*.

Anyway, Engel had been awake and watching. We both had a quiet giggle. The unknown Peter Taylor, who two days prior was deemed to have been the unknowing victim of selectorial homonomoeia, was by now a national hero, having picked up six wickets in an uncompromisingly mediocre batting performance from the English. He had been enjoined to chat to me on the programme, but when the producer rang in the morning he slammed the phone down. The pressures of instant stardom were apparently so great that he had even felt the need to go walkabout. Talk about overnight success! He does seem a very pleasant sort of fellow, though, and I do hope he does not end up, as so many do, just another three-day wonder.

Fortunately we managed to catch Australian wicket-keeper, Tim Zoehrer, instead: he of the limerick interchange with Phil. I heard through the grapevine that the producer had tried about four of the Aussies, and they had all refused. The general feeling was that I would give them a very rough time, and that this was a pain they could do without. They need not have worried. I am conscious of Australian cricketers' proclivities for bursting into tears, and would not have chanced so distressing a performance so early in the morning. Besides, at 7 a.m. I am a fairly harmless sort of creature, and it would certainly never have occurred to me, for example, to ask them whether they perceived themselves as a bunch of wimps for calling off their 1988 planned tour of the West Indies. At all events, interfacing with the West Indies and with La Edmonds appeared to rate equally highly on Australian cricketers' list of traumas to be avoided.

I believe, from Phil, that Tim was quite astounded that I could be so nice. Hell! Why on earth should I haul some poor blighter over the coals when he has been good enough to get out of bed to fill a colleague's spot? He made a few deprecating comments about Phil's ability to spin the ball, and we laughed about the limerick saga, a minor incident which the press, even serious broadsheets such as the Melbourne *Age*, are trying to turn into a mini-series; all in all it was fairly tame stuff.

'Yes, tame,' said old Engel. 'Most of the stories and interviews are so tame and trivial. And the stories are so trite.'

Engel, as usual, was incontrovertibly right. Stories on seals being weighed-in after Christmas, interviews which give folk three minutes to explain their life's work, or to expound on extremely complicated issues, cross-chat with half-witted actresses who are semi-speechless without a script – this is the stuff of which breakfast TV is made.

There were a few real gems that week, however, as for example an interview with the brilliant Spanish flamenco virtuoso Paco Peña, whom I have adulated since I first heard him in a one-man concert in Cambridge. But basically Engel was right. The good folk of Australia do not want to be hit with anything other than the anodyne at that time of the day.

It is almost inevitable, however (and the same goes for the chit-chat in the interpreters' booth once the microphones are switched off), that the conversation off-air – the asides, the commentary and the jokes – is far more entertaining than anything ever broadcast. The never-heard gloss that would be appended to stories on the set was far better value for money than the same old dreary autocue introductions. As I said, Gordon Elliot is a very funny man.

On the Wednesday of the week I was introduced to the astounding gastronomic phenomenon of the Great Australian Ginger-Nut. These biscuits have been keeping Australian orthodontists and dentists in car phones, skiing holidays in Gstaad, and houses in Double Bay for generations. It is impossible to break one with your bare hands. These small, round, brown discs could easily be used as an alternative to those heat-resistant tiles on space shuttles, or incorporated as one of the more lethal elements in a ninja's armoury. Plated together, they could easily be marketed as protective clothing for cricketers in the West Indies, or used by the building industry to provide indestructible high-rises along the San Andreas Fault. Strong men have been known to weep trying to crunch them, and it is common knowledge that black-belt karate experts would rather break a couple of hundred bricks than one Australian ginger-nut biscuit.

There is only one recognized mode of ingestion for the Australian ginger-nut. First it must be ceremoniously dunked in something hot, preferably a television station's inimitable machine-produced tea or coffee, soused for a few minutes until it becomes soft, and then quickly swallowed before the entire soggy mess disintegrates, like a heap of confectioner's mulch on your lap. Packets of the things were strewn ubiquitously throughout the set. The camera crew, who had been up since all hours, would use them for a quick sugar-fix. Gordon, who would choose a calorie-conscious lunch of Caesar's salad and soda water, would scrunch the dreaded ginger-nuts as if there were no arterio-sclerotic tomorrow. I never mustered the guts to experience one in between clips. As Gordon said, it was bad enough when I concentrated.

Bored with tales of handmade dolls' houses, and with people plugging themselves, we decided it was high time to make some mention of this great Aussie tradition, as quintessentially Australian as Vegemite, as imperturbably hard as Crocodile Dundee. On the Thursday, therefore, I composed an 'Ode to the Great Australian Ginger-Nut', and read it to Gordon before the programme.

'We'll do it,' he agreed conspiratorially.

'Shouldn't I square it first with the producer?' I asked.

'No,' said Gordon. 'He'll stop us.'

I, after all, was leaving the country shortly, and Gordon was leaving the show within ten days.

Fade-out came at 8.55 a.m., the scheduled item a musical snippet from Lionel Richie, who had already been inter-viewed on the programme.

Despite frantic signals from the floor manager we moved, as unstoppable as juggernauts, into our own 'nut' finale.

All over the country, good middle-class Australians, the 'disgusteds' from Mooney Ponds, the 'horrifieds' from Hamilton, and the 'speechless' from Sydney, erupted in a self-righteous orgy of myocardial infarcts.

By one minute past nine Channel 10's switchboard was in meltdown situation. The watchdog of Antipodean morals, the Australian Broadcasting Tribunal, was on the blower immediately, giving producer John Barton 'the worst day in my television career'. That is saying something. Barton was the unfortunate investigative film-maker who had been sacked by Alan Bond after his Channel 7 documentary on Queensland Premier Sir Joh Bjelke-Petersen, which eventually resulted in libel damages of half a million dollars.

What was it, well may you ask, that so incensed the population of a country whose projected image abroad is embodied by the Sir Les Pattersons, the Dame Edna Everages, the Paul Hogans, the Pamela Stephensons and the Dennis Lillees? Here, in unexpurgated form, unbowdlerized by a single syllable and brought to you by the unqualified broad-mindedness of William Heinemann publishers, is the verse:

> Our GMA* anchor man, Gordon,
> Kept dunking his nuts on the programme,
> When quite flaccid and soft
> He held them aloft
> Saying 'No man can cope with a hard 'un.'

Later that evening, during a moment's respite from the incoming calls, John phoned me to say it might be better if I did not bother to turn up for the final day. I was quite staggered at such a reaction to what was, when all was said and done, a piece of puerile *double entendre*. Let's face it, the limerick could have been taken either way. It taught

---

* GMA is *Good Morning, Australia*.

me a few salutary lessons, however. Never underestimate the prudery of a country which we Poms, often mocked for being the conservative one, have always perceived as a trifle brash and outrageous.† And never, ever, ever, sidestep a producer.

The team left to spend the weekend in Brisbane, and I invited two of the distaff team, Lindsay and Vicki, to Double Bay for lunch to celebrate my being banned from Channel 10.

Afterwards we said goodbye to Vicki, who was returning to sub-zero temperatures in England to help organize David's benefit season, and I returned to the Sebel to move the ever-increasing volumes of luggage into our next team abode, a block of self-catering service flats at Bondi Junction. There was a message waiting for me at the hotel. It was from Channel 9's top-rating programme *Willesee*. Could they come and film a day in the life of Frances Edmonds (all copyright on poetry reserved)? I suddenly remembered that this is the country where Jean Shrimpton scandalized the good burghers of the city by wearing a mini-skirt to the Melbourne Cup and, what was worse, failing to wear gloves and a hat.

And I recalled with a wry smile where that bit of controversy got her . . .

Two days later a huge floral arrangement arrived from Gordon, all pink proteas, carnations and, metaphorically, tortured willow with a message entitled 'The Ginger-Nut Crunch'.

> There once was a boy called Gordy,
> Whose remarks were exceedingly bawdy.
> Till his mate got the sack
> And he got a smack
> And the lawyers from Arnotts* said 'Tawdry'.

Dear old Gordon. I remember him with great gratitude and

† It was interesting that when Ned Sherrin read the piece out on BBC Radio Four's Saturday-morning *Loose Ends*, there was not a single hint of a complaint.
* Arnotts: ginger-nut biscuit makers.

affection. His new programme, an amalgam of hard news and current affairs, all melded together by Gordon's own irrepressible personality, is bound to be the success he made of GMA. It was all great fun while it lasted.

As luck would have it, my literary agent, Mark Lucas, of Fraser and Dunlop, was at the time on business in Sydney from London. He assured me that this minor débâcle, which had merely shocked the entire Australian nation, was really nothing to worry about and we could probably turn it into an 'earner'. I had already been to the first day of the Test at the Sydney Cricket Ground with a group of his suitably iconclastic mates. It is wonderfully soothing to be with people whose vaguely outrageous, under-grad sense of humour is consonant with your own.

Mark Hopkinson is a whizzkid merchant banker here at Schroders, Australia. He reminds me of my second brother, Brendan: extremely bright, a very dry wit, encyclopaedic knowledge on all sorts of unlikely esoteric subjects, constitutionally incapable of suffering fools gladly. We have now all decided that the only 'corporate-yuppy' way to communicate is over the car phone in the BMW, preferably in a traffic jam on the Sydney Harbour Bridge, whilst letting whomsoever you happen to be talking to know that you just have to hop out for a minute to pay the twenty-cent toll. I was suitably impressed to learn that Mark had swiftly sold all his New Zealand stock upon hearing the early-morning weather forecast one day on the car radio. The winds in Fremantle were about to favour Dennis Conner's *Stars and Stripes* against the Kiwis, who were fighting a last-ditch attempt to stay in the Louis Vuitton challengers final for the America's Cup. Sure enough, big bad Dennis romped home and, sure enough, the stock exchange in Auckland plummeted immediately. Until then the mystique of the money markets had always fascinated me. Suddenly I realized that such things are merely based on the way the wind blows.

By about lunch-time that day we were all feeling a couple of tinnies over par and rather peckish. No Swan Brewery hospitality box on offer here, I'm afraid. I went to scavenge and came up with an unlikely comestible reclining sluggishly in the pavilion bar's microwave. It rejoiced in the name of Chicken Hero, although whether this appellation designated the product or the protential consumer remains unclear. The Chicken Hero comes hermetically sealed in its own silver-foil bag, presumably for reasons of environmental pollution. I do not think that any putatively edible take-away has ever occasioned such ribald mirth amongst its consumers. This Hero is a long, thin roll, generously stuffed with a sort of mucous secretion which once upon a time might conceivably have been tangentially connected with a chicken. Then again, it might not.

Nick, Mark H's future brother-in-law, who along with Prince Edward has patently missed his vocation in the Marines, where men are men and sheep are scared, ate two. The rest of us had finished after one bite.

Australia, of course, went on to win the fifth and final Test, but there was far too much bad batting, bad bowling and bad umpiring to make it a truly great game. Nevertheless, if nothing else, the match demonstrated one point: two teams playing mediocre cricket can still prove genuinely exciting for spectators and players alike. A contest in which any one of three results remains possible until the very last minute, with the entire population of the Sydney Cricket Ground teetering on the brink of its seats until the bitter end, cannot be all bad. Besides, the match did evidence various aspects which were indicative of the series as a whole.

On the Australian side, Greg Ritchie, who in most people's books should be a permanent middle-order fixture in the team, was unfortunately forced to open the innings. A solid opening pair is a priceless asset in Test cricket, as England's Broad/Athey combination has shown. Indeed, much of the English psychological dominance in this series has stemmed from the stalwart performance of these two openers, and from the reciprocal fragility of their Australian counterparts, despite the often laudable efforts of an extremely professional Geoff Marsh.

All the more credit, therefore, must go to Dean Jones, who in effect, at number three, has often to all intents and purposes been opening the innings.

Jones's swashbuckling 180-odd at Sydney certainly established an excellent platform from which the Australians should have progressed. However, despite that, and some singularly exasperating lower-order partnerships, England still managed to bowl Australia out for 350. Jones has grown in stature and confidence as the series has progressed, aided by two stylish, if eventually redundant, centuries in the intervening Perth one-day challenge series, and it has been a joy to watch his development.

Allan Border has had a relatively quiet series for a figure of such international stature, but that was almost inevitable considering the intolerable media pressures to which he has been subjected since Australia's first-Test defeat in Brisbane. How England should thank the Australian press for its often vicious excesses. For all that, Border must still surely rank as the English bowlers' most prized scalp, and I know Phil rates his five Border dismissals in ten Border appearances as his own greatest contribution to the retention of the Ashes. Border's dogged century in Perth, allowing Australia to survive when a second successive defeat looked inevitable, was a brave captain's innings. I sincerely hope that this modicum of Australian success will at least serve to deflect some of the media flak from a man who, until recently, has had to play in a one-man band.

Peter Taylor, the overnight hero, was awarded the Man of the Match award, but for me the true highlight of the game was David Gower's first innings' effort, an impeccably beautiful gem. For the hundreds of thousands of cricket followers who hold the often misunderstood former England captain in great affection, it has been a treat to witness his gradual return to form this tour. After that lucky break in Brisbane, when he was dropped on nought, he has gone on to score over four hundred runs in the series, an aggregate surpassed only by Chris Broad, whose 487 at an amazing 69.5 average includes three consecutive Test-match centuries. It was certainly no more than his just deserts when Chris was acclaimed the Man of the Series.

Ian Botham's much-heralded exit from overseas Test occurred with more of a whimper than the usual bang. He too has had a quiet series in every possible way. His two vital performances, however, the one with the bat during his blistering century in Brisbane, and the other with the ball when he snapped up five wickets in Australia's first innings at Melbourne, give some indication of what we shall all be missing in the future. Only Bruce Reid of the Australian attack survived with any degree of stature from Beefy's merciless Brisbane onslaught, and it looks as if he will remain the fulcrum of the Australian attack for many years to come. There is, on reflection, no shortage of positive elements which could be galvanized into a very useful Australian side in the future.

As for England's Graham Dilley's return to form after years dogged by terrible injury, and Gladstone Small's remarkable success with the new ball, all go to show that the England team never has been, and most certainly is not now, a one-man show.

Wicket-keeper-batsman Jack Richards, brought into the team when the batting looked suspect early on, has proved himself a very competitive cricketer both behind the stumps and with the bat, particularly in his extraordinary century at Perth. Together with Mike Gatting in Sydney, he was almost instrumental in achieving a match-winning position. He took some magnificent catches in Melbourne, and the only memorable blemish on an untarnished record would be the missed chance of stumping Waugh at Sydney, which in the end proved crucial.

Spin-twins Edmonds and Emburey have also played an important role, tying down batsmen for hours on end, giving the captain time to take control of developments, and Embers' seven-wicket haul in Australia's first innings in

Sydney should by rights have been rewarded by something better than an England defeat.

At all events, with a two:one victory in the Ashes, and an astounding win in the one-day challenge series in Perth, England is looking like a reformed collegiate character. Whatever the outcome of the next one-day-knock-about-pyjama-game codicil to the tour, England will surely be returning home to a 1987 series against the Pakistanis a far more confident and aggressive side than the Johnsonian shambles they were quite rightly dismissed as being at the start of the tour.

It has not, however, been all lost Test matches, early-morning calls and being sacked from breakfast TV these last few weeks. Sydney is not a place that allows of depression. The rest day during the Test, for example, was anything but. David 'Fender' Gower and Allan Lamb, together with celebrated restaurateur Peter Doyle and the house of Bollinger, had ideas for the team which involved little in the way of relaxation. An alternative Test match had been organized at Doyle's piscatorial palace on the beach at Watson's Bay, between the MCC touring team and the 'Bollinger Belles'.

The inevitable tipple started flowing as soon as we boarded the Solway Lass schooner outside the Opera House, and set sail across the harbour. Elton John powered alongside us in a motor launch for part of the way, just to wave. I forgot to mention that he had carried a lucky charm into hospital with him when he was admitted for surgery. It was the pristine-looking bat Phil had given him after the Melbourne Test and, as most people noticed, barely used but for the a few red marks along the edges. How we all do hope that the op. has been a success.

The match started after a copious lunch, both teams replete with talent-levelling quantities of the company libation, and a surfeit of shellfish. The Bollinger Belles were comprised of Sydney socialites, television personalities (of whom I was still supposed to be one at that stage), journalists, wine representatives and a brace of beauty queens.

(Ian Botham had wisely elected to go elsewhere for the day.) Expatriate Pom, boxer Joe Bugner, was there as the Belles' minder, and his wife-cum-manager, Marlene, was nominated minder's minder. What a charming chap he is! Seated at the lunch table between Joe and Phil, I lurched over at one stage to replenish La Edmonds' glass with the necessary lotion. Long experience has taught me that ladies can remain thirsty for a very long time when Philippe-Henri is in charge of dispensing the drinks. A virtual non-drinker himself, except of course when England retain the Ashes, it does not readily occur to him that other people are in no way averse to the odd tincture from time to time. When I say from time to time, I do, of course, mean, on days such as this, more or less *all* the time.

'Please don't do that,' said Joe, relieving me of the bottle so voraciously clasped in my clammy little hand, and pouring out the requisite volume of the alternative amber nectar. 'You mustn't think boxers don't know their manners.'

I did not tell him it was not the boxers I was worried about.

The twenty-one defenceless Belles (aided and abetted by the fact that additional handicaps were continuously being introduced for the MCC team at the four umpires' discretion) played exceedingly well. There was quite a bit of blatant cheating, verbal abuse and intimidatory shouts from both sides, and the umpires seemed only vaguely conversant with the rules. Just like a proper Test match in Australia, really! Suitable, and indeed often unsuitable commentary was provided by Bob Willis, Norman May and Henry Blofeld, whose comments about Mrs Edmonds, legs open wide, waiting for a tickle, produced the inevitable raucous laughter. I had been elected Belles' wicketkeeper, since it is generally believed that I miss nothing. I did not know whether insult or compliment was intended, but it was widely suggested at the end of the day that Tim Zoehrer could not have done a better job.

The scorecard was maintained meticulously by Test

veteran Alan Davidson, and involved a few controversial decisions, such as:

Gower D., out for verbal abuse, for 6.
Broad C., out for obstructing a fieldslady, for 5.
Slack W., out for molesting an umpire, for 4.

The final score, thanks to a ten-to-one weighting system, was Bollinger Belles 250, English Lie-ins 61.

'Throwing-in' took on a new meaning when my own mode of dismissal had been effected by David Gower bodily transporting me into the raging surf and dumping me. After that, everyone went in; Blowers went in with his expensive camera still around his neck, and even Joe Bugner went in (although it took seven of the English cricketers and much accommodation from Joe himself to render that possible). Yes, everyone got well and truly soused. It was a very merry day.

A very merry day indeed and, more significant still, an index of the fact that it does not matter how you play the game, but whether you win or lose. All right, so England lost the final Test, but the tour so far has been an unexpected success. Imagine the blown Fleet Street or Wapping tabloid gaskets if the team had been involved in such a frivolous mid-Test outing during the last disastrous West Indian series. I can imagine the headlines now: 'Champagne Charlies in Frothy Frolics as Cricket-as-we-know-it Crumbles'.

The great British public does not care to have the dirt dug on a team perceived as national heroes, on cricketers lighting up the mid-winter misery and darkness by thrashing the ancient foe. One wonders whether consumers would have devoured the post-Windies shock-horror salacious stories with such gusto had we managed to win out there. In this ultra-professional cricket world, at least as far as media fall-out is concerned, we can all forget the eminently praiseworthy Corinthian ethic. As far as Joe Public's impressions of a team are concerned, the only thing that really counts is whether it comes up trumps.

We had already moved inexorably into the Benson and Hedges World Series Challenge when the *Willesee* crew, led by journalist/interviewer Neil Kearney, arrived at our Bondi Junction pad about 10 a.m. It is such a dramatic improvement, living in the normal confines of a flat, rather than trying to operate within the stiflingly claustrophobic restrictions of the average hotel room. Phil was in his favoured pose, recumbent on the couch like some sybaritic MCC pasha, staring fixedly at the box. The crew filmed the usual early-morning Edmonds' crossfire. Phil graciously admitted that I had helped him in his cricketing career, in that I generally ensured he left the house feeling angry and aggressive in the morning. They asked me what would I do if I found my husband had been touring around breaking furniture with faded Beauty Queens. I professed my deep-seated belief in the ancient Roman philosophy of *lex talionis*, an eye for an eye, and a tooth for a tooth. In common parlance that means I have met several men this trip with whom I would be only too happy to break a retaliatory bed.

'I always give tit for tat,' I countered, and, in the words of the immortal Sophie Tucker, 'there's got to be a lot of tat for what I've got to give.'

Phil went off to play in yet another of the preliminary one-day games against the Australians at the SCG. This one, incidentally, turned out to be a real cliffhanger, with Allan Lamb guiding England to a quite breathtaking victory by smashing eighteen runs off the hapless Bruce Reid's last over. Meantime the interview went on to cover such topics as my ideas on Australian men. Actually, I do not have too many ideas about Australian men, except that I do harbour this nebulous germ of an idea that few Aussie men are consistent with that macho-image so hyped abroad. I have said this before, and I am now more and more than ever convinced of its truth. Perhaps that image was apposite a few years ago when legendary tales were handed down of was it Dennis Lillee? or was it Rod Marsh? who held the record for the non-stop drinking of tinnies during an intercontinental flight from Australia to England.

Nowadays, if the advertisements are to be believed, all Aussie cricketers are probably on Diet Coke. I mean honestly, do *real* men drink Diet Coke?

The economy too would seem to indicate a certain lack of bullish behaviour in the country, although a Treasurer who suggests that Australia is on the brink of becoming a banana republic does little to harden anyone's currency. However, in stark contrast to the mawkish lack of self-confidence which obtains in other areas of endeavour, it is fascinating to watch the fearless entrepreneurial spirit of the Bonds, the Murdochs, the Packers, the Holmes à Courts and the Elliots at work. Although not all born Australians, they do nevertheless represent that gutsy and unquestioning belief in their own capacities which for me used to epitomize this brave, sometimes even brazen country.

Australian men? Why ask me? I do not believe in stereotyping any category of person on a nationality basis. Neither the men, nor indeed the women, of any particular country are necessarily an homogeneous bunch. What I do believe, however, is that the state of the national sport is often inextricably connected with the state of the nation. When the New Zealanders were doing so remarkably well in the America's Cup challenge series, for instance, the Kiwi stock exchange was looking rosy. The day they lost to the Americans and Dennis Conner, stocks took a nosedive. Similarly, a once-invincible national cricket team which now wimps out of facing up to the mighty West Indians in their own unevenly pacy and bouncy Caribbean back yard, would appear to be sadly indicative of a country whose once boundless self-confidence seems to have taken a temporary downturn.

In search of Australia's lost macho-man, we therefore set off to the celebrated R. M. Williams, Men's Outfitters, in Castlereagh Street, Sydney, where the sort of tackle a hardened bushman would need is on offer. It is all there. Your 'Drizabone' all-weather, waterproof overcoat-cum-macintosh, the moleskins, the sort of trousers you could chop wood on; the kangaroo-skin boots, which for less than

$150 dollars are designed to last a lifetime in the City, and many a punishing year in the bush. We bought one of the now-famous bush hats for Philippe-Henri, originally popularized by golfer Greg Norman, and the manager, Brad, informed us that they were selling like hot cakes since Hogan's appearance in *Crocodile Dundee*. Thanks to an article in some trendy New York fashion magazine, the 'Drizabone' was on offer in fancy Fifth Avenue boutiques for anything up to six times the Aussie price. There is an ironic twist, however, for any up-to-the-minute Yank who thinks he can walk around the streets of New York doing a 'Hoges' with impunity. Those of you who have seen the film will readily appreciate the rub. Chaps attracting attention on the streets by looking like the newest arrivals from Oz are being held up at knife-point, at the drop of an Akubra, by juvenile assailants out for kicks with flick knives, expecting their potential victims to pull a real knife. If the Sabatier-sharp artefact fails to materialize, then the chances are that the ersatz Aussies will be swiftly relieved of their snakeskin wallets. Crocodile Dundee lookalikes had better beware!

We arrived, camera crew and all, at the SCG just in time to see Phil take Allan Border's wicket . . . again. I have been giving this matter of wicket-taking some serious thought. A game as statistically orientated as cricket should surely be capable of finding some method of 'rating' wickets. It has always seemed unfair to me that an Allan Border wicket, or a Viv Richards wicket, wil go down against your name as one wicket, just the same as a Merv Hughes wicket or a . . . or a . . . No! Better not mention an English equivalent. I have to live with these people. I do feel, however, that on the basis of past performance, and current form, some cricket-loving bookmaker could work out such a rating, possibly on a scale from one to twenty. A Border, for example, would be worthy twenty points, and a good old Merv, say two. Bowlers with staggering reputations as leading wicket-takers might not emerge particularly well out of such as system. You hear it from the cricketers themselves. It escapes no one's notice how the ball cannot be prised from certain statistics-conscious bowler's hands when it comes to wrapping up the easy tail-enders.

Enough! When all is said and done, it is only a game, and anyway Phil's timing in presenting the *Willesee* team with the Aussie captain's wicket upon arrival could not have been better stage-managed. We presented him with his new tifter as he walked off the field, our low-profile-large-dimension captain.

Mike Gatting turned his eyes disconsolately heavenwards upon noticing the Edmonds ménage at the PR again. One can only assume that Phil should have sought Gatt's permission.

The team left for Adelaide the morning after that thrilling victory. There are so many of these one-day games, however, that there is no time to get excessively elated over a win, and no time to become excessively depressed over a loss. It must be difficult to be consistently competitive when there is just so much, even too much, cricket. How much Beluga can you eat? How much Bollinger can you drink? How many beds can you break? Eventually, everything reaches saturation-point.

For me, the dubious joys of the peripatetic cricket circuit have also, at least temporarily, reached saturation-point. After three months of packing and unpacking, of life in hotel rooms, I have had enough. It is a fool indeed who would readily leave Sydney, despite the vinous temptations of my Hardy's wine mates rest-day invitation to Reynella. And besides, the day of the boys' departure for Adelaide, I had even more prestigious fish to fry, in Canberra.

An invitation to address the National Press Club is, under any circumstances, an honour and a privilege, but for a Pommie woman to be asked to speak to this eminent forum during its Australia Day celebratory luncheon it is all the more so. It is daunting to see the photographs of immediate predecessors on the wall: outstanding politicians such as Margaret Thatcher, Rajiv Gandhi, Bob Hawke and Sir Les

Patterson; international diplomats, captains of industry and stars of stage and screen; famous authors and top-notch journalists. What on earth was I doing here?

The National Press Club in Canberra, as you would imagine, is comprised of members of the press corps, but visiting diplomats and local luminaries are also allowed to join. Only practising journalists, however, are allowed to exercise voting rights and to put questions to speakers. These are rules apparently designed to guarantee that the essentially press-dominated hallmark of the Club is maintained, since in some State press clubs the journalistic flavour has been over-diluted by extraneous elements gaining equal rights and taking over. No one is going to let that happen here.

Making your own vaguely amusing and perfectly fatuous speech is one thing. Fielding forty-five minutes of questions from the Canberra press corps is quite another. On winding-up my address, it was reassuring to be advised to remain good-humoured if a certain financial correspondent were to ask me an awkward question. This chap apparently boasts a healthy track record for pointedly rude questions to most speakers, or at least so I was warned. Sure enough, after the usual guff about life as a cricket widow, said journo stood up and asked a fairly detailed question about the EEC's trading patterns. Monetary Compensatory Amounts, the Common Agricultural Policy and the European Communities' budget.

There has never been a shortage of topics I can bore people to death with, but these are some of my favourite 'goodies'. I have, after all, been involved with European institutions since the United Kingdom acceded to the European Communities in 1973. It would appear I passed the litmus test. The putatively awkward financial correspondent even congratulated me on the answer – it was the only way anyone could think of to shut me up. He was the first, incidentally, to buy a copy of *Another Bloody Tour*.

From then on it was, as the saying goes, plain sailing. To this day I feel, however, that if I had fluffed there could have been carnage. I was, after all, dealing with the press, not the *a priori* perfectly well-disposed contingent which constituted the rest of the 350-strong audience. Someone asked for an interpreting anecdote. I ended up doing impersonations of Margaret Thatcher and President Mitterrand. Anything anti-French goes down very well here at the moment. The French Government, piqued in the United Nations over Australia's attitude to their neo-colonialism in New Caledonia, had recently kicked the Aussies' most senior representative off the island and there is currently even a retaliatory movement afoot to boycott French produce: no more Charles Jourdan shoes, no more Christian Dior clothes, no more French wine! They'll certainly feel the pinch! The Aussies, that is.

I returned to the now cricketer-free zone at our Bondi Junction apartments quite exhausted. It had been a long day. Lindsay Lamb, who is staying here with me for a few days before hitting the sunshine on the east coast, arrived half an hour later. It was definitely time for a well-earned flûte of something. We talked until late, our checking-up husbands interfering periodically from Adelaide to ascertain whether we were having a night on the tiles. Lindsay was incensed about a piece in one of the papers suggesting that Lambie had obstructed Reid during his mammoth final-over slog. We compared the column inches devoted to the unsuccessful Aussie cricket team and the column yards expended in high encomium on the wonderfully improved Aussie tennis player, Pat Cash. Even Hana Mandlikova has now been taken to the national bosom since she applied for Australian citizenship.

'These Aussies are not good losers,' said Mrs Lamb.

'These Aussies are a bunch of wimps,' hyperbolized Mrs Edmonds.

'Talk about Lambie cheating,' added Mrs L.

'Talk about cancelling their Windies tour,' rejoined Mrs E.

The hands of the clock moved forward. The meniscus of the bottle of whatever it was dropped. The opinions got progressively more bawdy. It was good to be out of the circus for a while.

When Lindsay left early, two days later, I missed her. It is comforting to know that you are not the only outrageous cricketing wife in the world and, despite well-proclaimed intentions of remaining in Sydney to write, her departure made me feel unconscionably depressed. It was therefore only 8.30 a.m. by the time I reached Palm Beach, and took up supine station in Hopkinson' hammock. The boy was doing the odd mega-yen deal on the blower to Tokyo. Nick, the future brother-in-law, was making chilli con carne for dinner. I looked at the cloud formation in the sky, the bright blue-and-black butterflies flutteringly fragile in the hydrangeas, the playful possum pottering in the pine trees, the cheeky kookaburras chortling merrily in concert, the surf thrashing with break-neck force on to the beach below. It was then with a sudden flash of incandescent lucidity that the thought crossed my mind: CRICKET XXXX CRICKET!

Try as I might to escape from its all-encompassing tendrils, however, what do I then behold in my half-hearted efforts to read the *Weekend Australian*, but that cricket supremo Jack Bailey, Secretary of the MCC, has returned from Australia after a nice cricket-watching hiatus in an English winter, and handed in his resignation. Up at Palm Beach, there was much corporate distress amongst the Pimms. Only two weeks prior, at a Double Bay dinner party, our brilliant physiotherapist hostess, Sarah, and our top trial-lawyer host, Russell, had sensibly but unnecessarily gone to great pains to place Jack and me at separate ends of a very long table. Without the restraining influence of celebrated peacemaker, Phil, it was generally felt that no one from Lord's would feel particularly comfortable within my immediate vicinity.

It was unfortunate, however, that they should instead have seated Mark Hopkinson in relatively close proximity to our now erstwhile MCC Secretary. Mark, an Oxford man and a northerner, has that wicked way with one-liners which so constitutes my idea of humour: a trifle sardonic, possibly, and often very pointed, yet never gratuitously malevolent. More and more he reminds me, as I have already said, of my brother Brendan, whose radical epistles to Jamaica's *The Gleaner*, berating the apparent indifference of the Seaga adminstration, will probably earn him a machete in the back of the head before he returns to the more tranquil climes of the Moorfields Eye Hospital in London later this year.

Seated on the other side of Jack was a friend of ours, Jane Adams, who deals with syndications for News Corporation Ltd, Rupert Murdoch's stable of newspapers here in Australia. From the bottom of the table, I could see a fairly animated conversation going on at the top. Wavy blond-haired head and wide blue eyes focused amiably on Jack, with all the innocent naïveté of a Botticelli angel, Hopkinson was asking what an MCC secretary actually did for a living. Did he, for example, send out receipts for the subscriptions, and take the gate money? Jack, by all accounts, was already finding some difficulty in fielding such questions, when Jane waded in, wondering whether being Secretary of the MCC was a full-time occupation, or whether it merely involved selling the odd egg-and-bacon tie on high days and holidays?

What on earth have they done between the pair of them? Has their genuine, if ingenuous interest precipitated an existential, nay nihilistic round of tortured soul-searching in poor Jack's red-and-yellow striped MCC bosom. Who will ever know . . . ?

10

The America's Cup

It was a wrench indeed to tear myself away from the idyll of Sydney, but who could resist an invitation to the swansong of the America's Cup?

Along with the majority of Australians, I too was disappointed when the people's hero, Alan Bond, the man who brought the America's Cup to Australia, was deprived of the right to defend it by Kevin Parry's Taskforce syndicate and the *Kookaburras*. In the challengers' final, despite some magnificent sailing in the preliminary rounds, the Kiwis had been decisively beaten by Dennis Conner, and most people had wanted to see a re-run of Newport – Connor's crew versus the Bondy boys. It was not to be, however, and already the final seemed a trifle second-best.

Both the Kiwis and the Bond syndicates had thrown the weight of their resources behind the *Kookaburras*, Bondy even handing over the Australian crew's totemic Boxing Kangaroo pennant to the cause, and they were thanked profusely by their syndicate director, Ken Court. Ken, of course, may well know plenty about twelve-metre racing, but his sense of history was ominously off course.

'When the Anzacs get together and put up a fight,' he said in a press statement, 'they usually win.'

Obviously no one had told him about Gallipoli. Obviously no one had told him about Big Bad Dennis.

197

It is difficult not to admire the irrepressible Bondy's ability to bounce back in the face of adversity. The day *Australia IV* lost the defence, he announced a multi-billion dollar take-over of Kerry Packer's Channel 9 media empire.

Lurking nebulously somewhere, there seemed to be a degree of bitter-sweet historical irony about the business. Kerry's father, Sir Frank, had been the first Australian to mount a challenge for the America's Cup and Bond had been the first Australian (albeit adoptive) to win it.

The portents for another Australian victory, however, were not good. For a start, Bob Hawke was out of the country on a middle-eastern tour. Had there been the merest sniff of an Aussie victory in the air, he would have doubtless been in Freo to greet it. So used are voters here to the Prime Minister's ubiquity at sporting successes, that Allan Border apparently refused to believe his much-maligned team had won the final Test until Bob walked into the dressing-room.

On yet another continent, the other PR politician, President Reagan, had woken up from his port-Irangate amnesia in time to wager his white cowboy hat on *Stars and Stripes* regaining the Cup for America. Members of the President's immediate entourage wondered what he would talk through should he be deprived of it, but with Conner three:nil up in a best-of-seven final, the chances of losing his normal conduit of communication seemed negligible. Ever game, Bob Hawke matched the bet with an Akubra on the *Kookaburras*, although wags were suggesting that Bond had added a codicil to the deal: if Parry's syndicate were to lose the Cup after all Bondy's herculean efforts to win it in the first place, the bush hat, it was mooted, would come attached to the head of the *Kooka III* skipper, Iain Murray . . .

I arrived at Perth airport to be met by a uniformed chauffeur in a white stretch limo, just the sort of vehicle American Presidents get assassinated in. He whisked me off to the Esplanade Hotel in Fremantle, where it was all happening. I had always thought cricketers attracted a fair quota of groupies, but this was an entirely different league of (as crew members refer to them so affectionately when they have served their useful purpose) 'star fuckers'.

Groupie-ism would seem to be an almost exclusively female preserve. Hordes of chunky young men, for example, do not tend to cluster around female tennis players; more likely, even there, to find hordes of chunky young women. But that's a different story. No, is it perhaps that *so* many women, for *so* many years, have been *so* used to gaining their names, their identities, their very social significance from the men they happen to be connected with that had produced this phenomenon? The sentiment of vicarious importance is so far deep-rooted that some women still patently feel that being bedded for the night by someone famous confers a degree of kudos.

For our sins, we had to suffer one such female over dinner in Perth last time we were here, basically because there are no depths to some otherwise quite acceptable guys' execrable taste. She claimed to be Franco-Swiss, but was about as Franco-Swiss as Kaiser Bill's batman. Not that there is anything wrong with being German, my word no, Not, that is, unless you are the sort of German who thinks it is better to be Franco-Swiss. Her multifarious claims to all sorts seemed tenuous to say the least, and it was difficult not to gain the impression that she was training for the decathlon in screwing. She had started on a few relatively low-profile long-distance runners, moved swiftly on to the more glitzy tribe of Formula One racing drivers, passed quickly through a couple of cricketers, and was now heavily into the twelve-metre men. Not bad, for a fortnight in Australia.

I remember talking to Jilly Cooper about this very phenomenon at a book launch last year, and she put her finger on the essence of it: again, the inequality of the sexes. The more successful or famous a man is, the more women he had to choose from, and the more fatuous females he has falling at his feet. The more successful or famous a woman is, the more isolated she becomes from men wary of her. That night at the Esplanade in Freo, there were wall-to-wall just such fatuous females, and all willing and eager.

Back at the World Series Cup, England seemed to be suffering from a mid-series crisis. An inspired piece of advice from Peter Lush had resulted in Botham opening the batting, a gamble which was paying off handsomely, and Bruce French, recalled to the team on Jack Richards's injury, was keeping wicket brilliantly. The middle-order batting, however, always an element of fragility in the side, was looking as stable as the Mexican economy. For a perilous while, the team seemed to have lost the will to win, and England's place in the final looked far from certain.

Never a mob to miss the right psychological moment, the Aussie crowd taunted on every possible occasion, especially as a revitalized Australian team had hammered England by 109 runs at Melbourne, and gained their rightful place in the finals. To add insult to injury someone had released a small wild pig on to the ground during the England innings, with GATTING daubed in white on the poor beast's side. The England captain had been caught for six off Waugh, and a joke immediately started to do the rounds. What was the real difference between Gatt and the pig? Answer: it was easier to catch Gatt.

In his defence, it would not seem that Mike allows himself to be in any way upset at such eminently personal jibes. During England's game against the Aussies in Brisbane, a hastily prepared banner had been held aloft adjuring: 'Mike Gatting. Ring Jenny Craig, IMMEDI-ATELY'. Jenny Craig runs a highly successful string of weight-loss clinics.

Poster-borne graffiti are certainly the art form most commonly on display in Australian sporting stadia, and although such exclamations as 'good shot', and 'wizard', or exhortations such as 'go for it' are depressingly banal, there is no shortage of genuine humour. The best example I have seen was on the centre court at the Australian Tennis Open at Kooyong, in Melbourne, during Australian Pat Cash's surprise defeat of Czechoslovakian Ivan Lendl. A young woman's poster read quite simply 'Cash beats a Cheque'.

In Fremantle, Dennis Connor, three:nil up in the finals, had decided to call a lay-day. The humiliations of Newport now seemed aeons away, and Dennis was enjoying himself. A few weeks earlier he had been taunting the opposition and the world's press with an ostentatious outing flying his new spinnaker, the 'Dolly'. Bequeathed to Connor by the New York Yacht Club when every other American contender had been eliminated, the Dolly was so-named for her numerous, large and ultra-curvaceous Parton-style projections. Dennis obviously felt confident enough to have some fun, and the Dolly was nothing but a red herring and a mickey-take. Ms Parton *à propos* is here in Australia, in majestic person, touring with a fellow country-and-western singer, Kenny Rogers. A prime mickey-taker herself, Dolly was once asked why on earth she continued to make such arduous tours when she was already a multi-millionairess.

Flashing those heavily be-false-eyelashed eyes from underneath the enormous platinum beehive wig, rustling the diamanté-tassled cowboy jacket stretched suggestively over the half-century bust, and wagging her sculpted finger-nails at the interviewer, she answered in that inimitable Tennessee drawl: 'Weyl . . . ya know . . . costs a lotta money ta look this cheap.'

The woman is priceless.

Since there was to be no racing that day, my hosts, Brendan and Pat Redden, some friends and I took a helicopter to the Leeuwin Estate winery and vineyard, located in the picturesque coastal resort town of Margaret River, some 280 kilometres south of Perth. The Estate is not only internationally recognized as a producer of premium wines, but also boasts a restaurant which won the prestigious Gold Plate Award at its first attempt. Despite fielding all the latest in modern equipment and technology, the winery nevertheless imports all its oak barrels from France for the wine ageing process, and no expense is spared in the tireless pursuit of small quantities of exquisite product.

The day slipped imperceptibly away in good conversation, good wine, good food and good company, and it was just as well we had our trusty chopper pilot to ferry us happily home. By that stage one of us subjected to a random breath test would have had a 1984 reserve bin Rhine Riesling, a 1983 Chardonnay, a 1982 Pinot Noir, and a 1982 Botrytis late-harvest Rhine Riesling to be taken down, and used in evidence against us.

The *Kookaburra*'s last-minute efforts to call another lay-day have been in vain. Today, Wednesday the fourth of February 1987, looks like staging the culmination of the America's Cup. The small town of Fremantle is bursting at the seams, and the short trip from Perth, which generally takes twenty minutes, is requiring a few hours. The gaily painted weatherboard façades have always looked somewhat two-dimensional, insubstantial, like a film set, and today the place looks more like Hollywood than ever.

The cast of thousands is predominantly Australian, but there is a fair contingent of Americans, some cheekily sporting T-shirts with the legend 'G'Bye. G'day'.

They, at least, are in no doubt as to which way the wind is blowing.

The famous Boxing Kangaroo, who, sporting his aggressive red boxing gloves three years ago in Newport, knocked the NYYC into a cosmic huff, is fluttering on pennants everywhere, but today lacks conviction, a bit like Dennis Andries after his drubbing at the hands of Thomas 'Hit Man' Hearns. As we wave the yachts off from the harbour he is even walking around in the flesh, or at least in the synthetic fur, and is no doubt silently grateful that there are no *Italia* crew members driving Alfa Romeos in the immediate vicinity.

It is only 10 a.m. and already the temperature is up in the high twenties. Papa Luigi's is full of Italians, taking their mid-morning fix of espresso. Eskies are hauled on to launches, stores of ice are being laid down, zinc cream is slapped on facial protrusions, choppers hover noisily above like so many sci-fi monsters . . . the America's Cup party is about to begin.

We have a choice. We can sail on a tender in the 'triangle', and seriously watch the racing, or we can sail on the *Leeuwin*, and seriously hit the vino. There is no competition. Besides, the *Leeuwin*, a magnificent traditional tall ship built to provide an adventure training facility for the youth of Western Australia, is equipped with several televisions, and if we get bored with the racing, we can probably watch some cricket.

The atmosphere at the starting line is sheer exuberance. Anyone who can patch his rubber dinghy with an Elastoplast is out here, jostling for a view. The Commodore of the New York Yacht Club sails past, looking snooty. A few drunken larrikins boo, and the sentiment is taken up in pockets. Dennis has become a folk hero here is Freo.

The rest is history. *Kookaburra III* never even got a look-in. No ferocious tacking duels, no fights around the marker buoys, no pan-national coronaries at the finishing line. *Stars and Stripes* romped home in a distressingly clean sweep.

Nevertheless, the scenes in Freo that night were positively bacchanalian. God knows what must have happened in Australia the night they won the Auld Mug. The Aussies were certainly having a riotous time losing it: people sitting in the gutter, arms around each other, supported by pyramids of dead tinnies; slurred versions of 'Waltzing Matilda' emanating from the favoured watering-holes, lyrics morosely changed to fit the occasion . . . 'And that was the end of the boxing kangaroo . . .'; dancing in the streets; Kookaburra sweat-shirts going cheap; one lone AIDS Jeremiah carrying his lugubrious message on a sandwich board, unheeded by an unashamedly hedonistic crowd.

The presentation ceremony was an emotional event, even for those who were not commensurately tired. The Commodore of the Royal Perth Yacht Club, Alan Crewe, handed the America's Cup, glistening in the brilliant sunshine, to the Commodore of the San Diego Yacht Club, Fred Frye. Frye, in turn, presented Crewe with a bicycle spanner, the implication being that the spanner, of metric design, would be virtually useless in wresting the trophy from the San Diego Yacht Club where the Cup would be secured by imperial bolts. True to his end of the bargain, Bob Hawke had ensured that the American President's bush hat was entrusted to Conner, for delivery on his return to a rapturous ticker-tape welcome. It was unfortunate, however, that the Prime Minister had not seen fit to append instructions. Subsequent photographs showed the Irangate-beleagured Ronnie wearing the titfer back to front.

Conner, by now an unofficial roving amabssador for Western Australia, could not have been more gracious in victory. The folk of Freo have taken him to their hearts in a way the NYYC never did. When asked where he would like to see the next challenge held, he answered unerringly 'Fremantle', and was duly rewarded with an affectionate cheer.

Watching the last of the sailors leave, the Western Australian talent must have felt like so many Didos saying farewell to beloved Aeneases, not quite managing to stave off the sinking feeling that this could be adieu rather than *au revoir*. They were not yet sufficiently forlorn to light the funeral pyres, however. After all, Bondy had promised to go and get that Auld Mug back . . . again . . .

The next day I left for Melbourne, just as an exclusive liner was sailing into Fremantle. Guests on board were each paying a few thousand dollars a day for accommodation, but it was worth every red cent. They had saved up to come all the way from New York to watch the final of the America's Cup!

11

Grand Slam

There was a strange, white laundry bag sitting in the bedroom on my arrival at the Menzies at Rialto, Melbourne. On further inspection it revealed its contents: a life-sized doll's head, with a very large open mouth attached to an ingenious pumping device. Phil, it transpired, had won the Wanker of the Series award.

England, despite concerted efforts to screw everything up, have made it through to the best-of-three finals of the Benson and Hedges World Series Cup. This, more than anything, is due to the fact that they have come upon a team which atypically 'can't bat, can't bowl, and can't field' even more effectively than themselves. Yes, the mighty West Indians, tactically bankrupt, and psychologically deflated and depressed by the continuing veto on bouncers in one-day games, have been eliminated. The finals will be the old foes, England versus Australia.

The prospect of a Grand Slam has obviously given England that final fillip of which they were so desperately in need. By this stage, however, there is no shortage of bitching starting to surface, especially amongst the side-lined members of team. It would appear that the only players who are regularly obliged to pitch up at practice nets are the ones who have absolutely no chance of playing in the actual matches. It might not have been bad policy, under the circumstances, to oblige the *entire* team to practise. Goodness knows, some of the middle-order batting performances, in particular, were sufficiently catastrophic as to warrant the odd work-out.

Much as I would have loved to witness the nets-niggling for myself, I was sadly obliged to fly off almost immediately to Brisbane, to address a Lord's Taverners' luncheon. Ex-Australian cricket captain and current selector, Greg Chappell, was there to give the vote of thanks. He is certainly one of the most suave, impressive and sophisticated chaps, impeccably well-mannered and -dressed, and heavily into the soda water at lunchtime. He is, by all accounts, now demonstrating an interest in moving into politics, having pursued a very successful career in real estate, and speaks disturbingly highly of Sir Joh. It will be interesting, however, to see which party, if any, he finally embraces.

It was a delight, too, to meet that remarkable old man, Ray Lindwall. As with Tiger, I seem to have a much greater affinity with the ex-s and the formers than with current-day cricketers.

A revivified England won the first final in Melbourne, and the circus rolled ebulliently back to Sydney, although at this stage no one was entirely sure which day it was nor indeed exactly where we were.

We were staying once more at our Bondi Junction apartments, where Ian Botham, along with his new Worcestershire team-mate Graham Dilley, had taken the penthouse suite. Sensing a two:nil England victory, Elton John had organized a party there for the evening of the second final. There is nothing that concentrates cricketers' minds on success like the prospect of packing for the thirty-first time, and taking an early flight next morning back to whence they have just come.

It was already nearly midnight when England arrived back at our Sydney sojourn. Day-night fixtures tend to roll on until about 10 p.m. in any event, and then the usual round of presentations, press statements, triumphant toasts . . .

I had been hard at the tripe-writer all day, and for once was not feeling like a party. Phil, however, who had only played in one of these limited-overs fixtures, decided we had better put in an appearance. 'Otherwise,' he said, 'they'll all say I'm pissed off about not playing.'

The wicket that day at the SCG, as indeed the wickets everywhere else with the possible exception of Adelaide, had turned square, but England had resolutely fielded three seamers and just the one spinner, John Emburey. The truth of the matter was that PHE was indeed pissed off about not playing.

I suppose we stayed about an hour. As usual with Elton, it was a generous and lavish do, with an enormous barbecue and buffet, courtesy of the Sebel Town House, ubiquitous red, white and blue balloons, and plenty of good bopping music. Sober, unfortunately, I get bored very quickly, and foolishly we left.

Oh, serious error! How is it I always seem to miss the action? If tabloid tales of unknown ladies wearing nothing but miniscule tank tops are to be believed, we were back to Caribbean standards at last . . .

Let us not dwell on minor casualties such as ransacked lifts and dismantled ceilings, however. If elevators malfunction, leaving Dennis Lillee immured airless and lightless, suspended for hours between Ian Botham's penthouse and eternity, such things are wont to happen.

Neither let us dwell on the fact that as a direct consequence of this, a healthy contingent of the team, including Les Edmonds, was summarily decanted into other establishments around Sydney early the next morning. No, such are the vagaries and vicissitudes of life in a touring party, and certainly none of these peccadillos was going to spoil the general euphoria in the England camp or the British nation, where a spate of post-Falklands gung-ho chauvinism had apparently taken grip of the land.

Just as we were moving our possessions for the thirty-somethingth time, however, the phone rang, and a man operating under the code name of 'Bill' from the British

Consulate-General in Sydney asked specifically to speak to me. Would I, a mere cricket widow, take delivery of a telegram from the corridors of power back home in London?

It did seem a trifle odd, to say the least, but I nevertheless agreed, promising faithfully to guarantee delivery to the manager. It had, after all, been the same Peter Lush who had encouraged me to write the piece in *The Times* diary, criticizing the Prime Minister and the Sports Minister, Richard Tracey, for their failure to send congratulatory telegrams when England retained the Ashes. 'Not that it will make any difference,' Peter assured me. 'Probably nobody reads your diary anyway. Certainly I don't.'

Oh, naughty, naughty Peter, to get poor debutante hackette Frances E. into such diplomatic hot water. When I returned home to England, it became perfectly clear why 'Bill' was at such pains to ensure that I saw the telegram arrive. Back in London, amongst the shoals of unopened mail, envelopes looking like bricks full of American Express counterfoils, invitations to appear in court over unpaid parking fines, and Christmas cards from people who know us so well they had assumed we were in the UK for Christmas, was a very official wodge of an epistle from the Department of Transport and the Environment.

'Dear Mrs Edmonds,' (it ran)
'I have come across several references in the press to the failure of the Minister for Sport to send congratulatory telegrams to the team during their hugely successful tour of Australia, stemming I suspect from your Sporting Diary article in *The Times*.'

(That was reassuring at least. Even if real punters like Peter do not read the wretched column, at least the other organs of the press plagiarize it.)

'This is a trifle irksome.' (Oh, dear, the Minister is irked.)
'Mr Tracey sent four telegrams, the first on retaining the Ashes, the second on adding the Perth challenge, the

third on the first victory in the World Series Cup, and the fourth on the second and the grand slam it brought with it.' (Copies of the same were duly enclosed.)

The missive continued:

'I enjoyed your reflections on the West Indies tour. This of course is simply in the interest of accuracy, should you wish to refer to the matter of the telegrams in any account you may record of the Australian tour!'

Dear, dear, dear! The Ministry of Transport and the Environment had patently decided that a roving Mrs Edmonds was a serious Governmental pollutant. The Minister had indeed sent the telegrams, the first one to Perth about a week after the Ashes victory in Melbourne. I wondered whether the Minister had had to be reminded of the fact in the intervening period. But, does it really matter? David Owen of the Social Democratic Party was first off the mark anyway.

The majority of the team was to fly back to England at the weekend, although Gladstone, Lamby, Embers, Jack and Both had made alternative arrangements. Phil and I elected to go to Hamilton Island on the Great Barrier Reef for a week's post-tour R and R, and flew up on the Friday with our 'dear old thing', Blowers.

This island was purchased a decade ago, on a long lease from the Queensland Government, by entrepreneur Keith Williams. Keith, a wonderfully extrovert man, is one of the major developers to have opened up the Gold Coast to the tourist industry, and is now devoting his boundless energies to turning Hamilton into the 'most desirable tropical island in the world'.

The major attraction is, of course, the proximity of the reef, where imperceptible hours can easily be spent scuba diving and snorkelling, dazzled by the underworld infinities of coral formations and fish. Nearer to shore, all the usual water sports are also available, as well has hang-gliding and para sailing.

Keith invited us out on his super-charged speedboat, *Awesome*, which it most assuredly is. It takes him all of three minutes to do a tour of the island, pointing out ex-Beatle George Harrison's villa as he goes.

A modern-day Prospero, Keith orchestrates the island entirely along his own lines. Early on, in a joint venture with Ansett Airlines, he created a landing-strip out of nothing, and nowadays all but the largest jumbos may put down there. He oversees every development with the eye of a benevolent dictator. 'Anyone can build anything they want here,' he claims, 'so long as I like it.'

He is currently winding up negotiations on the construction of two first-class hotels, which should give a further boost to the influx of tourists. At the moment, most of the accommodation is in self-catering apartments, with the option of eating at any one of the resort's dozen excellent restaurants.

It was a relief and a release to be off our own 'today-is-Friday-it-must-be-Sydney' tour, and fascinating to watch the collegiate behaviour of other people's. A healthy contingent of Japanese had just flown into Hamilton, though not quite so healthy as the state of their ever-hardening yen against an ever-depreciating Australian dollar. They were all, of course, extremely polite, and were all, of course, earnestly intent on learning the noble art of scuba diving in a mere two-hour session at the swimming pool . . .

The morning after our arrival on the island, after a superb lobster-and-mud-crab dinner in the 'Outrigger' with Blowers and Peter and Pauline West (Westie, just retired from the BBC, has been covering the tour for London's *Daily Telegraph*), Phil and I took the chopper up to the reef for a look at the sub-aquatic action. Apart from us, everyone else flying up the reef that day was Japanese, and there were a few minor linguistic problems. There was one of them who seemed to have some vague notions of the English language, presumably picked up from a Berlitz teacher with a very pukka accent. This, however, was doing him absolutely no good in his efforts to communicate with indigenes operating in the English-based patois commonly referred to as 'Strine'.

As we were leaving at 11 a.m., and returning at 3 p.m., our driver to the heliport thought it wise to advise us that there would be no lunch provided. I thought this a superfluous piece of information. Surely no one in his right mind would have expected an otherwise ubiquitous Big Mac outlet to be glistening brightly, red and white, on the Great Barrier Reef?

Our Japanese friend with the vague notions of English had patently been elected team interpreter, and jabbered something quickly to his uncomprehending mates. Goodness knows what the misunderstanding was, but before you could say 'Sony Walkman' they had all disappeared, to return ten minutes later, each bearing twice his body-weight in club sandwiches and hamburgers. Phil and I shared a helicopter with four of their number, Phil very sensibly sitting in the front and chatting to the pilot, and I very quietly sitting in the back, watching their diminutive frames forcing down these vast quantities of fodder.

In charade-type gesticulations, I did my best to convey the impression that stuffing oneself with convenience food immediately prior to a forty-foot submersion was possibly not the most sagacious course of action. They thought I was very funny, filmed my Jacques Tati effects on their video cameras, and offered me some chicken nuggets.

It was a glorious day out on the reef, not a cloud in the sky, but the strong wind creating quite a swell. The instructor gave us each a handful of bread, with which to attract the multitudes of fish feeding on the reef. Some distance away I could see Phil, arm outstretched, totally encompassed by swarms of bright blue chrome fish, gaily striped sergeant-majors and duller, but eminently more edible-coral trout. It was a wonderland of multicoloured corals, brain-shaped, stag-horn-shaped and fungus-shaped. The shoals of fish, in no way inhibited by the presence of humans, came up to us unabashed and cheekily nibbled at our fingers in their efforts to relieve us of the Hovis. The blistering sunshine refracted dazzlingly through the water. The only sound was that of your own breathing. Such tranquillity. Such peace. it was then I felt the shadow of a large body fall across me. It was a shark . . .

Back at the pontoon, the last of the samurai were busily puking their hearts out. No matter, it was all good biodegradable stuff, quite a well-balanced and finely masticated diet of first-rate protein and carbohydrates, and the fish were lapping it up. It is, however, very difficult to be properly sick whilst trying to maintain 'face', to hang on to a pontoon in a twenty-five-knot wind, to empty the 'Fairisle' chunder from your mask and mouthpiece, to balance two heavy oxygen tanks on your back, and to look interested in what the semi-anglophone interpreter is giving you by way of advice from the instructor. The unblemished white porcelain complexions of the ladies, incidentally, had sprouted a distinct green willow-pattern design . . .

It was not a very large shark, about five feet from toothy-looking jaws to tail, but then again I am not a very fast swimmer. Story of my life. All style and no stamina. I had heard stories about divers thumping sharks in the eye, but on the other hand I thought it better to let him make the first move. No point aggravating him unnecessarily. It was nice to think still in terms of 'other' hands. Perhaps soon I would not have that luxury.

My life flashed before me in a second. It seemed to contain an awful lot of empty bottles, and a couple of unfinished books. Not much for the obit columns to work on there. I wondered whether Phil would demand a refund on the return half of my chopper fare. I did not feel the cold fingers of panic grip my stomach, just the dreadful sense of irony that I should be sloughing off the mortal coil to feed a fucking fish.

Suddenly, as if from nowhere, our instructor appeared, and the shark turned its belligerently carnivorous attentions on him. Now, I am as full of the milk of human kindness for my fellow man as the next woman, but I could not help but see this as anything other than a very definite step in the right direction. The two were within inches of one another, seasoned diver and five-foot sharkette, when the instructor lifted his arm. Whoopee! Perhaps a swift right hook to the snout, that would teach the blighter a lesson . . .

The next thing was the perfectly incredible spectacle of the black be-latexed diver and the white-tipped coral reef shark muzzling one another affectionately. The pet shark, Sophie, was completely harmless and, even if she wasn't, she had so much to eat on the reef that she certainly wouldn't be bothered with tough old boots like me. Or so they assured me, a full thirty seconds later as, traumatized, I reached the pontoon in true Dawn Fraser style, not to be enticed into the water again that day.

12

Pillow talk

There comes a time in every married woman's life when she feels the need to do something totally out of character, something she would subsequently rather forget, something she might be too ashamed to admit even to her best friend. It is more than often due to the not uncommon sentiments of frustration, loneliness and boredom. Modern psychologists sometimes refer to this phenomenon as the 'Talking to the Husband Syndrome' or THS for short.

Perhaps it was simply a case of delayed shock. Loquacious at the best of times, the confrontation with the shark had thrown me into severe verbal overdrive. So bad did it become one day that I was even moved to talk to Philippe-Henri. I had to. He was the only person in bed with me at the time . . .

The Derby and Joan of the England team, we are, by now, old hands at this touring lark: the joys of success in India, the mortification of defeat in the West Indies, the phoenix-like renaissance of the team in Australia, we have seen it all.

More than anything, of course, it was interesting to discuss the essential differences between the disastrous Windies tour last year, and the triumphant march through Oz less than twelve months later. There can be no doubt that Australia proved much tamer opposition than the West

Indies, especially in the bowling department. In the Windies there were the likes of Marshall, Garner, Holding, Courtney Walsh and (particularly in Jamaica) Patrick Patterson, constantly assailing the England batsmen with 'throat balls' and giving the Windies a marked psychological dominance from the outset. Even as early as the island match against Jamaica, before the first Test, their pacemen were out to undermine England's confidence. We both remembered the spectacle of Walsh coming in to bowl against David Gower, and visibly moving up several gears in a definite attempt to frighten England's prize scalp. In the dressing-room everyone took heed of the warning so clearly being issued: there was to be plenty more of this to come.

The effect of this on England, apart from completely understandable bouts of the Caribbean equivalent of Montezuma's Revenge, was an almost immediate disintegration in morale. As a consequence of anticipating the worst, batters, even top batters, got it firmly lodged into their heads that they would inevitably receive the unplayable ball at some stage. They therefore felt that they absolutely *had* to play shots in between those unplayable balls. Nobody was prepared to play 'à la Boycott', to hang around, to stay there, to wear the fast bowlers down, and to try to hit any bad ball that came their way.

The rest is history. In the first Test in Jamaica, playing on a variable wicket, the fast boys just annihilated England, most of the English batsmen going down playing shots. That, along with Gatting being smacked in the face in the one-dayer, reinforced the general apprehension for the rest of the tour.

Therein, if anywhere, lies the major difference between the two tours – the state of the Englishmen's minds. In Australia, despite some very lacklustre performances in the State matches, particularly against the Aussie left-armers, it was obvious that the Australians were never going to dominate England psychologically, and neither were the

English batsmen ever going to feel uncomfortable against the sort of pace they could generate.

From then on there were various lucky windshifts which served to pull England out of their doldrums. Gower being dropped on nought in the first innings in the first Test was perhaps the most crucial turning-point. He went on to make fifty-odd, which overnight lifted him out of his own personal crisis. And then, of course, there was Botham's blistering 138 in the same match, which completely restored England's shattered confidence in their own abilities, and engendered the general feeling that four hundred runs should always be possible against that sort of attack.

A few inspired pieces of advice had also helped matters along. Until then, I had never known that it had been Phil's idea in Brisbane for Gatt to move himself up the batting order to number three. Early on in the tour, the opening batsmen were looking a bit dicey, and David was struggling at that position. Phil argued that Mike had always done a good job for Middlesex at number three, and should in the circumstances be trying to do the same here in Australia, with David at number five. The new permutation worked wonderfully well, helped by the fact that the opening partnership, the combination England had striven so hard to find, also came good.

Here again the difference between England and Australia was fundamental. Broad and Athey soon melded together to form an extremely solid opening pair, and their stability provided an excellent platform on which other stroke-makers could build. The Aussies, on the contrary, were in trouble for most of the series, with Boon so badly out of nick. The Australians were constantly chopping and changing in increasingly more desperate efforts to find an acceptable batting line-up, whilst England had the luxury of consolidating into a well-balanced squad.

This line-up was in marked contrast to last tour's 'hokey cokey'-style team. Because the batting was so positive in Australia, England could afford to play five genuine bowlers, with a balanced attack of three seamers and two spinners. The two spin-twins, Edmonds and Emburey, accounted for a good fifty per cent of all the bowling, which meant that England had long periods of control in the field. In the West Indies, on the other hand, England, in ever more frantic attempts to shorten a tail which refused to wag, were obliged to slot in the extra batsman at the expense of a specialist bowler, and the mere memory of Viv Richards smashing a century in about half an hour at Antigua is sufficient commentary on the wisdom of such a four-bowler approach.

Success, naturally, feeds upon success in the same way defeat feeds upon defeat. Moods and attitudes, for better or for worse, tend to infiltrate the entire team. The England batsmen were feeling good and this rubbed off on the bowlers. Dilley in particular went from strength to strength. He started off with five wickets in Brisbane, and gradually perfected those outswingers to become a genuinely top-class bowler. DeFreitas, too, did well in Brisbane, and when Gladstone was suddenly given his chance in Melbourne, he grasped it with alacrity.

Man-management, too, has undergone a welcome change since last year's tour. In fairness to England's management in the Windies, it is clearly easier to manage a buoyant and successful team than it is to manage a disheartened, disaffected side. The unfortunate Tony Brown was trying to deal with a team who were being massacred on the pitch and flagellated in the press, and half of whom were making no secret of the fact that they did not want to be on tour in the first place. At least there was none of that kind of nonsense for management to contend with this time.

It would be quite wrong, however, to suggest that this management team did better merely because external circumstances were easier. In effect, even in absolute terms, they did a far more professional job. This was probably due, in no small measure, to the fact that every member of the management in Australia had a specific job, a well-defined remit, and an awareness of the confines and the boundaries of his competence. Micky Stewart, for instance, was 'cricket manager'; he dealt specifically with everything appertaining to cricket. Last year Bob Willis's job was always completely vague, and it was difficult not to feel a trifle sorry for him when he ended up as little more than a glorified baggage manager.

Mickey had certainly played a major role in the team's organization. When England lost in Brisbane in the State match before the Test, for example, it was he, not the captain Gatt, who led the short postmortem. If David had had that sort of counsel and support in his day, there is little doubt he would still be captain of England now.

Good old 'Fender'. He certainly was never one to go overboard about the value of externals. When hammered by the press in Antigua for failing to insist that the team should practise in unplayable conditions (the 'cow patch' was the woefully apt appellation of the nets), his reply was quite simply, 'If you want cosmetics, go to Boots.'

At the time, I had thought that an inspired *bon mot*: smoke presumably emanating from his ears, P. B. H. May had not.

No, David never really saw the value of public relations, a discipline based more not on doing the right things, but on being *seen* to do them. Micky, on the contrary, had a very shrewd idea of the value of externals. In Australia the team was always on the field at 10 a.m. for an 11 a.m. start, ostentatiously running, sprinting and stretching while the spectators and press were supposed to be filtering in. (I use the word 'supposed' because most of the press would in fact be watching proceedings on the television from the comfort of their hotel rooms until TV coverage stopped, when they were positively *obliged* to go to the ground.) The point is that DeFreitas, Dilley and Botham had already been in the nets bowling their hearts out since 9.15 a.m., a patented recipe for pulling a muscle – bowling first and stretching later. Nevertheless, it was imperative to do the physical jerks whilst everyone was at least *thought* to be watching.

Of course, it is easy to act the overtly professional part

at Australian grounds, where facilities are second to none. Although the early-morning aerobics were basically for public consumption only, practice arrangements, with plenty of enthusiastic club players and excellent net bowlers putting the team through their paces, were extremely useful. Subsequently, when the team was on a winning streak, and everyone was trying one hundred per cent, just about everything on the field looked good. England's catching and fielding, for example, were never better.

The greatest triumph of the entire tour, however, and for once Phil and I were in total agreement, would have to be the unsung hero, manager Peter Lush. His personality and common sense have been the bulwark of the team's success. I, for one, shall certainly treat the next 'scoop' he gives me with the deepest suspicion, but when the bouquets are being handed out for this Grand Slam victory, he deserves the largest.

By this stage, Phil had started to give me yet another ball-by-ball account of his five Allan Border wickets, and his strained groin muscle in Sydney. I fell asleep instantly. Meanwhile, somewhere over Heathrow, a British Airways flight fron Sydney was stacking to land, and England's victorious cricket team were preparing for a rapturous welcome.

Epilogue

1. England retained the Ashes and won the series 2:1
2. England won the Benson and Hedges Challenge
3. England won the Benson and Hedges World Series Cup
4. Dennis Conner and *Stars and Stripes* won the America's Cup
5. Alan Bond took over Kerry Packer's Channel 9
6. Rupert Murdoch took over the *Herald and Weekly Times*
7. William Heinemann Australia were granted permission to publish Peter Wright's memoirs. The decision went to appeal, and Heinemann won
8. Malcolm Fraser never did find those trousers

Tom Sharpe
Porterhouse Blue £2.50

To Porterhouse College, Cambridge, famous for rowing, low academic standards and a proud cuisine, comes a new Master, an ex-grammar school boy, demanding Firsts, women students, a self-service canteen and a slot-machine for contraceptives, to challenge the established order – with catastrophic results . . .

'That rarest and most joyous of products – a highly intelligent funny book' SUNDAY TIMES

Riotous Assembly £2.50

A crime of passion committed with a multi-barrelled elephant gun . . . A drunken bishop attacked by a pack of Alsatians in a swimming pool . . . Transvestite variations in a distinguished lady's rubber-furnished bedroom . . . Famous battles re-enacted by five hundred schizophrenic Zulus and an equal number of (equally mad) whites . . .

'Crackling, spitting, murderously funny' DAILY TELEGRAPH

The Throwback £2.50

'The tale of an illegitimate member of the squirearchy earning his inheritance by increasingly nasty methods – gassing, suing, whipping, blowing up, killing, stuffing – is both inventive and pacy' NEW STATESMAN

'Black humour and comic anarchy at its best' SUNDAY TIMES

'A savage delight' DAILY MIRROR

Tom Sharpe
Ancestral Vices £2.99

'Left-wing academics, right-wing capitalists, true blue country gentry, workers, peasants, police and lawyers – all take custard pies full in the face in this boisterous knockabout farce' LISTENER

'Another bawdy and brutal romp of the kind he does so well' NEW STATESMAN

'Takes us at a gallop through the whole repertoire of British jokes' AUBERON WAUGH, EVENING STANDARD

Blott on the Landscape £2.50

'Skulduggery at stately homes, dirty work at the planning inquiry, and the villains falling satisfactorily up to their ears in the minestrone . . . the heroine breakfasts on broken bottles, wears barbed wire next to her skin and stops at nothing to protect her ancestral seat from a motorway construction' THE TIMES

'Deliciously English comedy' GUARDIAN

Wilt £2.99

'Henry Wilt works humbly at his Polytechnic dinning Eng. Lit. into the unreceptive skulls of rude mechanicals, but spends his nights in fantasies of murdering his gargantuan, feather-brained wife, half-consummated when he dumps a life-sized inflatable doll in a building site hole, and is grilled by the police, his wife being missing, stranded on a mud bank with a gruesome American dyke' GUARDIAN

'Superb farce' TRIBUNE

' . . . triumphs by a slicing wit' DAILY MIRROR

Clive James
Unreliable Memoirs £2.95

The Kid from Kogarah tells all.

'You had better not read the book on a train, unless you are unselfconscious about shrieking and snorting in public! OBSERVER

'The public's favourite wit and pundit, reduced in imagination to short-trouser size, wrestling with snakes and aunties and mutual-masturbators in the bush-bordering suburbs of postwar Sydney . . . called up in the familiar two-fisted prose. The old boy may be forty, but he times a punch-line disgustingly well'
RUSSELL DAVIES, LISTENER

Flying Visits £3.50

' . . . a riveting mix of wit, humour, satire and above all, penetrating observation' IRISH INDEPENDENT

'Following Mrs Thatcher around China, dazzling a posse of Russian hotel maids with his ability to say, "The bath illuminations have been destroyed", rocking the slipstream of Washington's joggers, he is a sympathetic traveller and a shrewd pinpointer of the funny, frightening, surreal or otherwise significant detail' OPTIONS

'James is the ideal common viewer, with whom we rejoice to concur' LONDON MAGAZINE

Visions Before Midnight £3.50

TV criticism from the *Observer* 1972–6

The first selection from the newspaper column that made TV criticism an entertainment in its own right. The 1972 and 1976 Olympics, *War and Peace*, the Royal Wedding, the Eurovision Song Contest, the exit of Tricky Dick – the favourites are all here.

'Clive James's television reviews . . . turn the pale glimmers on the set into something like a gaudily lit portable theatre of clacking wooden puppets . . . his stunning pieces readjust horizontal and vertical holds almost before there is time to blink away the images that were actually transmitted' DENNIS POTTER

All Pan books are available at your local bookshop or newsagent, or can be ordered direct from the publisher. Indicate the number of copies required and fill in the form below.

Send to: **CS Department, Pan Books Ltd., P.O. Box 40, Basingstoke, Hants. RG21 2YT.**

or phone: 0256 469551 (Ansaphone), quoting title, author and Credit Card number.

Please enclose a remittance*-to the value of the cover price plus: 60p for the first book plus 30p per copy for each additional book ordered to a maximum charge of £2.40 to cover postage and packing.

*Payment may be made in sterling by UK personal cheque, postal order, sterling draft or international money order, made payable to Pan Books Ltd.

Alternatively by Barclaycard/Access:

Card No.

Signature:

Applicable only in the UK and Republic of Ireland.

While every effort is made to keep prices low, it is sometimes necessary to increase prices at short notice. Pan Books reserve the right to show on covers and charge new retail prices which may differ from those advertised in the text or elsewhere.

NAME AND ADDRESS IN BLOCK LETTERS PLEASE:

....

Name ——————————————————————————

Address ——————————————————————————

——————————————————————————

——————————————————————————

——————————————————————————

3/87